Aphrodite
Goddess of Modern Love

JOHN KRUSE

GREEN MAGIC

Aphrodite Goddess of Modern Love© 2021 by John Kruse. All rights reserved. No part of this book may be used or reproduced in any form without written permission of the authors, except in the case of quotations in articles and reviews.

Green Magic
Seed Factory
Aller
Langport
Somerset
TA10 0QN
England

www.greenmagicpublishing.com

Designed & typeset by Carrigboy, Wells, UK
www.carrigboy.co.uk

ISBN 978-1-7399733-0-8

GREEN MAGIC

Contents

Introduction	5
Background & Origins	6
Inanna & Ishtar	6
Astarte	8
Cyprus & Greece	9
Aphrodite Arises	11
Birth	12
Fertility, Sex & God Time Girls	13
Lovers & Children	19
Conjugal, consensual, concupiscent?	20
Aphrodite's Girdle	21
Aphrodite in Art	22
Rome	24
Diversity	25
Sacred Sex	28
Ecstasy	38
Aphrodite & Mary	39
Odes to Aphrodite – Poetry	41
Sappho	41
Robert Herrick	44
Nineteenth Century Verse	47
Dante Gabriel Rossetti	52
Æ (William Russell)	53
Arthur Rimbaud	55
Madison Julius Cawein	59
Richard Le Galliene	62
Ernest Dowson	63

Algernon Swinburne	65
Marina Tsvetaeva	72
Clark Ashton Smith	73
Stevie Smith	78
W.H. Auden	81
Sylvia Plath	83
Geoffrey Grigson	84
Conclusion	86
The Goddess in Prose	87
John Donne	88
Pierre Louys	91
Aphrodite	92
The Songs of Bilitis	110
Louys – An Afterword	119
Sader Masoch, *Venus in Furs*	120
"Strike Dear Mistress" – Hymns to Venus	124
"Venus in her naked glory" – The Goddess in Art	130
Francois Boucher	131
Nude Venus in the Victorian Art	134
Symbolist Goddesses	141
Expressionist Eros	145
Salvador Dali	147
Paul Cuvelier	151
Conclusion	156

Introduction

> "The sap of Spring in the young wood astir,
> Will celebrate with green the Mother,
> And every birdsong shout awhile for her;
> But we are gifted, even in November
> Rawest of seasons, with so huge a sense
> Of her nakedly worn magnificence
> We forget cruelty and past betrayal
> Heedless of where the next bright bolt may fall."[1]

This book is about the goddess of love, Aphrodite – or Venus, or Astarte – she has had many names. She is the goddess of life, fertility and renewal, but she is also the patroness of carnal desire: "a thousand honey secrets thou shalt know" is her promise to the boy Adonis in Shakespeare's poem about the pair. Incredibly, perhaps, he resists this offer – but most of us do not.[2]

> "From the beginning she has been honoured
> And apportioned among the immortal gods and men
> With conversation between girls, and deceiving smiles,
> And sweet delight and love and gentleness."[3]

The enduring role of the goddess in human sex and passion is well known, but what I want particularly to examine here is how well she may be suited for love and sexuality in the modern world – how, in fact, an ancient goddess is still a highly relevant goddess for our time. To understand that, we must trace something of her origins, before focussing our attention on the way in which more recent writers and artists have imagined her.

---

[1] Robert Graves, *The White Goddess*.
[2] Shakespeare, *Venus & Adonis*, line 16.
[3] Hesiod, *Theogonia*.

Background & Origins

To understand the roles and meanings of Aphrodite in the modern world, it is helpful to understand something of her origins. These can be traced as far back as the beginning of settled human civilisation, in the form of fertility goddesses who oversaw the fecundity of crops, livestock – and their human keepers. At some early point, too, the goddess of sex also became associated with war.

INANNA & ISHTAR

The first clearly identifiable antecedents of the modern Aphrodite appear in Mesopotamia and the Levant, the goddesses Inanna, Astarte and Ishtar. These deities can be represented by statues of fecund women with ample thighs and plump vulvae, often proffering their breasts to the worshipper, but they can be found too as slender young girls or as small-breasted teenagers, impetuous, flighty, fickle and desirable, yet all of them capable of bringing death as well as life-engendering sex.[1]

A Bronze Age prayer to Inanna, dated to about 2500BC sets out the varied benefits that the deity brings. These are, as just mentioned, both love and war, but they include too all aspects of religion, monarchy, politics, civilisation and agriculture:

> "The dagger and sword... the quiver...
> The art of lovemaking... the kissing of the phallus...
> The art of prostitution... the cult prostitute...
> Rejoicing of the heart... procreation..."[2]

---
1   B. Hughes, *Venus & Aphrodite*, 2019, 18 & 20.
2   D. Wolkstein & S. Kramer, *Inanna, Queen of Heaven & Earth – Her Stories & Hymns from Sumer*, 1983, 16–18.

BACKGROUND & ORIGINS

Inanna (also called Ishtar in Akkadian) was the Sumerian Lady of Heaven linked to the planet Venus and, as the prayer has shown, presiding over all matters of love, beauty, sex, war, justice and political power. She was a virgin mother-goddess, a figure of great power and devotion. The rites of her worship seem to have had some distinctive sexual aspects. Her priests were known as *gala* and seem often not to have identified with traditional male roles. They sometimes adopted female names and speech forms and, in addition to their duties celebrating the goddess, they would have sex with male worshippers. Equally, at the Sumerian New Year, the king participated in a ceremony in which he ritually married the goddess and then had intercourse with the high priestess.[3]

The cult of Inanna/Ishtar has long been thought to have involved sacred prostitution, although some scholars now doubt this. 'Hierodules' (holy women) known as *ishtaritum* worked in Ishtar's temples, but it is unclear whether or not these priestesses actually performed any sexual acts as part of their religious duties (although Hammurabi went to the trouble of enacting laws to protect their reputations from slander, which might imply that there was cause for malicious gossip about them). Nonetheless, as we shall see, at some later date sacred prostitution certainly became a key part of the worship of Innana's descendant, Aphrodite. She also seems to have inherited her companion doves from her Sumerian antecedent.

Amongst Ishtar's lovers was Dumuzi (also called Tammuz). He was either her brother or, even her son, another early indication of the sort of sexual liberality that will come to mark the cult of the goddess throughout the ages.

---

[3] Worship of the 'Great Mother,' Cybele, was also celebrated with orgiastic rites by eunuch priests dressed as women and called '*gallli*.' The goddess herself was said to be both male and female.

ASTARTE

In the Levant, in the lands inhabited by the Phoenician peoples, Ishtar became Ashtoreth or Astarte (Atargatis in Syria) and was the principal goddess of the seasons and of fertility, functions which included supervision of the sheep flocks and being patroness of hunters. She was associated too with fish and with doves and was linked to the moon. In statues she may be seen crowned with a crescent moon and, not infrequently, triple breasted.

Astarte had important temples dedicated to her at Sidon and Tyre and shrines are known too at Ashkelon and Jerusalem. She was 'queen of the heavens' but also earth mother and lady of the seas. One of her symbols was the phallus and sex and sexuality were closely associated with her worship, being expressions of natural growth and fertility. Today, any sort of worship that involves sex seems alien to us, but in ancient times intercourse was seen very differently: it was a public and sacred function. Ceremonies in Astarte's temples included wild dancing, drunken ecstasies and the ritual deflorations of virgins.

In due course Astarte travelled west with Phoenician explorers and, in Carthage in North Africa, was worshipped as Tanit. This goddess appears to have been something of a reversion to more primal views of an elemental earth and sea mother, a sinister mistress who demanded child sacrifice. She remained, in addition, a celestial or lunar goddess and was represented by a disc and crescent symbol. The cult also travelled down the Nile, with a Phoenician temple to Astarte (also called 'Aphrodite the Stranger') established at Memphis.[4]

---

4 G. Herm, *The Phoenicians*, 1975, 197.

CYPRUS & GREECE

In time, the cults of Astarte/Ashtaroth travelled across the Mediterranean Sea to Cyprus – and, in fact, the goddess long retained a particular link with the sea and with water. Among her many honorary titles were *pontia* and *pelagos* (of the sea), *euploia* (smooth sailing), *galenaia* (of the calm) and *limnaia* (of the harbour). These associations and attributes have lasted right into the present.

On Cyprus, the Phoenician goddesses encountered existing fertility goddess worship and a fruitful interaction took place between the two. At Paphos, on the southern coast of the island, one of Aphrodite's principal shrines was established. Herodotus relates that it was Phoenician colonists from Ashkelon who founded the temple, but it could very well have been built at a place where a local 'mother goddess' had been celebrated previously. The sanctuary was walled about and contained gardens and ponds as well as the temple itself. The site came to be renowned across the Mediterranean, but there were at least half a dozen temples to the goddess on the island, as well as important subsidiary shrines to be found on Cythera, Crete and Sicily. On the latter island there was a major shrine on Mount Eryx, where Aphrodite had seduced the mortal male Anchises. She was worshipped here as *Venus Erycina*; in time, the Romans carried off her statue from the Phoenician temple and set it up in Rome, where the goddess was thought to be especially sympathetic towards prostitutes and 'common girls.' It's known that prostitutes (as well as 'respectable' women) were involved in celebrating festivals at the various Roman temples to Venus.

D.H. Lawrence painted a picture of this Sicilian shrine, which he visited in 1921, drawn like a pilgrim by the ancient stories of the goddess, the 'Laughing One of Mount Eryx':

"And the hill near us was Mount Eryx. I had never seen it before, so I had imagined a mountain in the sky. But it was only a hill, with undistinguishable cluster of a village on the summit, where even now cold wisps of vapour caught. They say it is 2,500 feet high – still, it looks only a hill.

But why in the name of heaven should my heart stand still as I watch that hill which rises above the sea? It is the Etna of the west ... To men it must have had a magic almost greater than Etna's. Watching Africa! Africa, showing her coast on clear days. Africa the dreaded. And the great watch-temple of the summit, world-sacred, world-mystic in the world that was. Venus of the aborigines, older than Greek Aphrodite. Venus of the aborigines, from her watch-temple looking at Africa, beyond the Egatian isles. The world-mystery, the smiling Astarte. This, one of the world centres, older than old! and the woman-goddess watching Africa! *Erycina ridens.* Laughing, the woman-goddess, at this centre of an ancient, quite-lost world...

I confess my heart stood still. But is mere historical fact so strong, that what one learns in bits from books can move one so? Or does the very word call an echo out of the dark blood? It seems so to me. It seems to me from the darkest recesses of my blood comes a terrible echo at the name of Mount Eryx: something quite unaccountable. The name of Athens hardly moves me. At Eryx – my darkness quivers. Eryx, looking west into Africa's sunset. *Erycina ridens...*

A different goddess the Eryx Astarte, the woman Ashtaroth, *Erycina ridens* must have been, in her prehistoric dark smiling, watching the fearful sunsets beyond the Egades, from our gold-lighted Apollo of the Ionian east. She is a strange goddess to me, this Erycina Venus, and the west is strange and unfamiliar and a little fearful, be it Africa or be it America."[5]

---

5   Lawrence, *Sea & Sardinia,* 1921, c.2.

BACKGROUND & ORIGINS

Aphrodite Arises

It was during the eight century BCE that the goddess received her new name. She had initially been referred to simply by the titles 'The Queen' or 'The Goddess,' but these labels were displaced by *Kypris* (in other words, the goddess of Cyprus) or Aphrodite. The origin of the latter is still disputed: *aphros* in Greek means the foam of the sea, and a legend exists explaining how she was born from the foam generated when her father, Ouranos, was castrated and his severed organs fell into the ocean. This, though, may be a back-formation from the name, an explanation worked out in ancient times for a mysterious appellation. It is very possible, in fact, that Aphrodite is just a Greek attempt at pronouncing Astarte or Ashtoreth or some other unfamiliar Phoenician name; we know for a fact that the Greeks struggled with the name of Astarte's close cousin, the Syrian goddess Atargatis, which they transformed into Derketo.

As well as a new name, the goddess also acquired a number of new epithets, such as *pasiphaes* (shining on all), *asteria* (starry) and *urania* (heavenly) which clearly indicate a celestial origin, if not a lunar one. These titles are just the beginning. Aphrodite was also known as *peitho* (the persuader or enticer), *epistrophia* (the heart turner), *psithyros* (whisperer), *parakyptousa* (the sideways glancer) and *machnitis* (the one who contrives – that is, to bring couples together). Love and attraction hopefully lead to partnership, so that Aphrodite was also *nympha* (goddess of brides), *harma* (the one who joins or unites), *thalamon* (of marriage beds), *praxis* (of successful outcomes – when in bed with a lover...), *charidotes* (giver of joy) and *paregoros* (comforter). She was also *apotrophia*, 'the expeller,' because she expels desire from our hearts after pleasure and lust.

Birth

The image of Aphrodite being born from the sea is an abiding one (another of her epithets was *Anadyomene*, meaning 'rising from the sea') and Botticelli's famous painting of the *Birth of Venus* attests to the myth's power, at the same time becoming an icon in its own right. Botticelli shows a slim, adolescent beauty being blown by the Zephyrs towards the shore, standing on a scallop shell, white roses wafting around her in a breeze as an attendant awaits to wrap her in a flowered gown. The scallop refers to her oceanic origins, but it also symbolised the female sexual organs and was worn by devotees of the goddess' cult as a mark of their allegiance. British poet Geoffrey Grigson even went so far as to claim that Venus' "peculiar expression" in this famous painting was that of a woman during an orgasm. I'll let readers decide on that.[6]

We're all familiar with the oceanic birth seen in the famous painting but, because she is a composite goddess who has been inherited from several earlier Middle Eastern cultures, the Greek Aphrodite in fact has several natal stories. The truth is that even our image from Botticelli, of Venus surfing ashore on her shell, is a more modern imagining of the ancient myth. Older tradition represented her being born from between the open valves of the scallop – and some sculptures also show her emerging from the shell holding her father's severed penis, doubling up the genital iconography of the image. This is underlined in Plautus' play *Rudens*, which is set in and around a temple to Venus at Cyrene in Libya. Two young girls who are devotees of the goddess are referred to as *conchas*, 'shells,' which is very likely to be a *double entendre* referring both to their faith and to their gender. Likewise, 'the cleft meadows of Aphrodite' is a phrase from Empedocles which needs no elaboration...[7]

---
[6] Grigson, *The Goddess of Love – The birth, triumph, death and return of Aphrodite*, 1976, 21.
[7] Plautus, *Rudens* (211 BCE), Act 3, Trachalio.

Other genealogies abound. Homer recorded that Aphrodite was daughter of Zeus and the earth goddess Dione. Latin author Gaius Julius Hyginus reported a Syrian account in which she was hatched by doves from a large egg that fell from heaven. Even on Cyprus, where she is supposed to have come ashore, there were other stories: for example, that she was just a local girl – born at Aphrodision, brought up at Kythrea and known to bathe in a spring near Khrysokhou – in between bouts of sex with Akamas, Athenian hero of the Trojan wars. Italian Renaissance poet, Ludovico Ariosto (1474–1533), knew this last story and celebrated it in his epic *Orlando Furioso*. He described a voyage to Venus' isle, "land of love and languorous delight" and a visit to the so-called *Loutra tis Aphroditis* ('Aphrodite's Bath'):

> "Here for her rule the goddess has full scope,
> Here is her bower, here she had her birth.
> Here are fair women, nor let any hope
> To find them equalled anywhere on earth.
> Both young and old, they burn with ardour more,
> To Venus subject till their dying hour."[8]

Evidently, this visit would appear to have been more than just sightseeing – but then, we would expect sailors to have a girl in every port, in true veneration of Venus.

Fertility, Sex & God Time Girls

> "Oh! shed a favourable glow both on my love and on my ship, Cypris, you who reign supreme on the lovers' bed and on the shore of the sea."[9]

In Homer's *Iliad*, supreme deity Zeus stated that the tasks of Aphrodite "should be making marriages, embracings, kisses,

---
8 Ariosto, *Orlando Furioso,* Canto 18, verses 136–139.
9 Epigram by Gaitoulikos, *Anthologia Graeca*, 5.17.

charms." So it was to be; although Hellenicised and made respectable by incorporation into the pantheon of Olympus, Aphrodite remained fundamentally a deity of fertility and, as such, she was associated still with flocks (of rams and billy goats but also of deer) and with birds (doves, geese, partridges, swans and sparrows). These creatures all seem to have been selected for their lustful reputations. Underlining this, it appears, one image of the divinity was the *Aphrodite Epitragia*, which showed her astride a billy goat.

The goddess was also particularly linked with fruit and flowers (for instance poppies, cypress, roses, myrtle, quince and pomegranate). She was called *antheia* (the goddess of flowers) and she oversaw gardens, the arrival of spring and plant growth, as well as birth, marriage and family life. Ultimately, she was the goddess of *mixis*, of mingling – whether of bodies or of the earth, water and sky.

The red rose is the flower most emblematic of the goddess and it is intimately associated with her. According to one story, roses sprang from the blood of Aphrodite's lover, Adonis, when he was gored to death by a boar. Another legend relates how she created the red rose, by walking across a bed of white roses and injuring her feet on the thorns so much that her blood dyed the petals: hence William Drummond of Hawthornden (1585–1649) imagined Aphrodite, the "Idalian Queen" (that is, from Idalium on Cyprus):

> "Her hair about her eyne,
> With neck and breast's ripe apples to be seen,
> At first glance of the morn
> In Cyprus' gardens gathering those fair flowers
> Which of her blood were born..."[10]

---

10 Philostratos, *Letters About Love*; Drummond, *Madrigal: 'Like the Idalian Queen'*.

In consequence of her associations with reproduction, sex was definitely never far away from Aphrodite's cult. If sex between the gods encouraged fertility, copulation between humankind could both praise the gods *and* encourage the processes of fertility in the natural world. One of Aphrodite's major shrines existed at Corinth and was apparently well staffed with prostitutes to entertain pilgrims. Items excavated on site show that both gay and straight sex were available within the temple grounds. These pleasures came at a price, though. Roman poet Horace wrote that *"Non cuivis homini contingit adire Corinthum"* ('Not everyone gets to go to Corinth'). What he meant by this was explained later by grammarian Aulus Gellius: one especially notable Corinthian courtesan, Lais, was available to visitors, but only for ten thousand drachmae a visit, an enormous sum.[11]

By this time, too, Aphrodite had been completely divorced from any association with warfare,[12] as the seventh century BCE *Homeric Hymn* to the goddess shows. It contrasts her to martial Athena, Artemis and Hestia, who are unimpressed by the "lover of smiles" and who remain immune to her charms. All the other Olympians, though, she leads astray into lovemaking with humans; such is her power, in fact, that her sheer presence can even inspire animals to mate. She is, moreover, renowned for her "sweet laughter," although this is a further *double entendre*, as it is another metaphor for the labia. This is made very clear by an episode in Lucian's *Erotes*, during which some friends visit the temple of Aphrodite at Knidos. They admire Praxiteles' famous statue of her, one of them exclaiming appreciatively:

> "what a well-proportioned back! What generous flanks she has! What a satisfying armful to embrace! How delicately moulded the flesh on the buttocks, neither too thin and

---

11 Horace, *Epistles*, vol.1, xvii, line 36; Gellius, *Noctes Atticæ*, 1, 8.
12 An *Aphrodite Areia* (warlike), who was clad in armour, was honoured in Sparta though.

> close to the bone, nor yet revealing too great an expanse of fat! And as for those precious parts sealed in on either side by the hips – how inexpressibly sweetly they smile!"[13]

So bound up was she with sex that, in classical Greek, the deity's name acquired various sex-related derivations, such as *aphrodiastikos* (lecherous), *aphrodisia* (brothels) and *aphrodiazein* (to copulate). Aristophanes called wine 'Aphrodite's milk,' for very obvious reasons.

Sex and passion are entwined with every aspect of Aphrodite's cult. Her temple at Knidos was surrounded by a garden of myrtles, cypress, bay and other fragrant trees. Lucian also informs us that, hidden discretely within the foliage, there were 'pleasure benches' and 'pleasure booths,' where couples who had paid their respects at the goddess' altar with incense and flowers could then express their devotion in other ways. The Latin text, *Pervigilium Veneris*, 'The Vigil of Love,' is set at a temple of Venus on Sicily where similar love booths, woven from myrtle branches, were set up: "tomorrow in the shade of the trees will the Joiner of Loves entwine the green huts of myrtle stems." At a spring festival, virgins would be summoned by the goddess to be taken to bed for the first time:

> "She, with her gem-dripping finger enamels the wreath of the year;
> She, when the maid-bud is nubile and swelling winds – whispers anear,
> Disguising her voice in the Zephyr's – 'So secret the bed! And thou shy?'
>
> Misdoubting and clinging and trembling – 'Now, now must I fall? Is it now?'
> Star-flecked on the stem of the brier as it gathers and falters and flows,

---

13 Lucian, *Erotes/Amores*, para.14.

> Lo! its trail runs a ripple of fire on the nipple it bids be a rose,
> Yet englobes it diaphanous, veil upon veil in a tiffany drawn
> To be-drape the small virginal breasts yet unripe for the spousal of dawn;
> Till the veined very vermeil of Venus, till Cupid's incarnadine kiss,
> Till the ray of the ruby, the sunrise, ensanguine the bath of her bliss;
> Till the wimple her bosom uncover, a tissue of fire to the view,
> And the zone o'er the wrists of the lover slip down as they reach to undo.
> Now learn ye to love who loved never; now ye who have loved, love anew!"[14]

This particular translation, by Sir Arthur Quiller Couch, is somewhat fevered and overwrought in tone and diction, but the focus on breasts permits a small detour. One of Aphrodite's sacred fruits was the quince, the choice being made – it would appear – because of the perceived resemblance between the flower buds and nipples and between the ripe fruit and bosoms. Poet Leonidas of Tarentum described Apelles' painting of Aphrodite new-born from the sea: "With beautiful grace does she wring out her hair with her finger-tips, beautifully does calm love flash from her eyes, and her breasts, the heralds of her prime, are firm as quinces." Greek jurist Solon advised newly-weds to eat quinces before their first night together, for the benefit of their aphrodisiac effect.[15]

On the Acropolis in Athens there was another shrine to the goddess. According to the geographer Pausanias, during the four yearly Panathenaic festival, virgins called *arrephoroi*

---

14 Lucian, *Erotes/'The Affairs of the Heart,'* para.12; Sir Arthur Quiller Couch, *The Vigil of Venus,* 1912.
15 Leonidas, *Anthologia Graeca,* 16, 182.

(bearers of 'unspeakable things') would carry baskets containing sacred objects from the main Parthenon plateau down to a cave in the grove of Aphrodite beneath the hill. We are left to speculate what these unspeakable items may have been, but one suggestion is that they may have been loaves, baked in the shape of snakes and phalli, which were a symbol of sexual awakening. Carried to the shrine, they would have received fertilising power from the deity, which would then have been disseminated by crumbling the bread into seed grain.

Meanwhile, the ceremonies performed at Aphrodite's temples on Cyprus and Cythera seem to have come straight from the Phoenician homeland. The temple offered prostitutes to worshippers and the rites were orgiastic – "degraded by repulsive practices" as one authority wrote. During the annual festival of Aphrodisia there was feasting, dancing and singing. Young girls were ceremonially deflowered and young men would visit the holy harlots to be initiated into the ways of the goddess, going home afterwards with a small model phallus and a lump of salt in their hands, symbolising sex and the sea-born deity. Commerce went with the pilgrims, including slave markets offering for sale Cypriot girls who were famed, allegedly, for their sexual prowess. It's hardly surprising, then, to learn that another bye-name for Aphrodite was *Porne*, the whore.[16]

Given this bawdy reputation, Plato sought to differentiate between two separate aspects of Aphrodite – between *urania*, the stern heavenly mother goddess who oversaw marriage, and her younger, earthier, more vulgar side, who believed in free love and was worshipped with bodies, not with flowers and incense. It was this common Aphrodite who came riding on a goat, a clear symbol of her wanton character. This dichotomy is probably a false one, for we must accept that Aphrodite was a complex character with multiple facets.[17]

---

16 Grigson reports even more explicit epithets, such as Aphrodite 'the hole,' 'who rides astride' and 'who opens up' – *The Goddess of Love*, 117.
17 Plato, *Symposium*, 180.

Lovers & Children

Aphrodite was a goddess with many lovers. Some were other Olympians, including Hephaestus, Ares, Poseidon, Hermes and Dionysos. Some of her partners were mortals, such as Anchises and Adonis. According to certain reports, the latter was just a young teenager, barely able to grow a beard, when Aphrodite took a fancy to him. Shakespeare describes him as "unripe" when he attracts the goddess' attentions but, given that Adonis was born from a myrtle tree, there was probably no escaping his fate.[18]

As many as sixteen children came from these relationships, fully justifying Aphrodite's role as 'divine mother.' Amongst others, the goddess bore the beautiful Hermaphroditus, who we shall discuss later, and the malformed Priapus, his oversized penis nevertheless being highly suited to the son of such a mother: in one of his poems Theocritus remarked how Priapus had "such splendid tackle for doing Aphrodite's work."[19]

Eros (Cupid) was another of these offspring and almost certainly one of the most important. In the most ancient Greek myths, Eros was one of the very earliest deities, son – perhaps aptly – of Chaos.[20] Hesiod described his effect upon us when he called him:

> "the dissolver of limbs, subduer
> Utterly of wits and sense of every
> God and all mankind."

This early Eros came bearing a torch (to ignite the flames of passion) as well as his notorious bow and arrows.

It was much later tradition that made him son of the love goddess and granted him multiple manifestations, the minor

---
18 Shakespeare, *Venus & Adonis*, lines 127 & 524.
19 Theocritus, *Idyll,* 15.
20 Perhaps this is why Aphrodite is blamed for precipitating the Trojan War, through her interference with Paris and Helen.

divinities called the 'Erotes.' These are the retinue of semi-divine beings that accompany and assist Aphrodite. As well as Eros, there are six other Erotes, who are named Anteros ('requited love'), Hedylogos ('sweet talk'), Hermaphroditus ('hermaphrodite'), Himeros ('uncontrolled desire'), Hymenaios ('wedding hymn') and Pothos ('desire or longing' – especially for an absent lover). The Erotes were seen as winged male youths and, in their role as the demi-gods of love and sexual desire, they used to be invoked to win or keep lovers; equally, they might punish those who rejected love. For that matter, according to Elizabethan playwright John Fletcher, "Venus will frown if you disprize her gifts/That have a face would make a frozen hermit/Leap from his cell and burn his beads to kiss it."[21]

To summarise – for Aphrodite, promiscuity was good and full of virtue. She took many partners and if her devotees did so too – prostitutes with many clients, clients with many prostitutes – the world was enriched by their loving (think of Wilhelm Reich's 'orgone').

Conjugal, consensual, concupiscent?

Familiarity with monotheistic religion leads us to assume that gods have to be perfect and infallible. The Greeks never made the mistake of demanding such defects of their pantheon. All the Olympians were flawed and Aphrodite was one of the least faultless of all. As we have seen, she had many lovers and many children, but she was a poor mother and a worse spouse. A popular story concerning the goddess was her affair with Mars whilst she was still married to Vulcan. Zeus had insisted that the pair should be wed and Venus resented this, so throughout their marriage she carried on an adulterous relationship with the god of war. Her husband suspected what was happening and several

---

[21] John Fletcher & William Shakespeare, *Double Falsehood, or the Distressed Lovers,* Act, scene 2.

times tried to catch the pair together. Eventually he forged a very fine metal mesh in which he trapped them in bed – and then exposed them to the ridicule of the other gods. Tintoretto and Parmigiano are amongst many artists who portrayed these scenes.

Despite her own unwilling match, Aphrodite had no hesitation about imposing her desires on others when she wanted them. Neither Adonis nor Anchises, her mortal lovers, were consensual partners – but she had sex with them anyway. It should also be remarked that those mortals who slept with the goddess always tended to have grisly deaths at a young age.

The goddess could be inconstant as a lover and untrustworthy generally, a person whose word was not to be relied upon. One of her names is *Apatouria*, meaning 'the deceitful.' This derives from an incident when she was attacked by giants and called Heracles for assistance. He hid himself with her in a cave and, as the giants approached her one by one, she surrendered them to Heracles to kill. Another of her names was *gameli*, the overseer of marriage – spectacularly inappropriate in the circumstances. Her uxorious qualities are entirely overshadowed by her physical passions.

Aphrodite's Girdle

Another sexualised aspect of the goddess was her belt or girdle, a thin strip of material that ran between her breasts and around her torso. Her power over human hearts is symbolised and assisted by this item, termed a *zone* or *kestos* in Greek and *cestus* in Latin. According to Homer, the girdle was where:

> "all enticements to delight, all loves, all longings were,
> Kind conference, fair speech, whose power the wisest doth enflame."

The girdle had an irresistible effect, giving beauty, grace and elegance, even when worn by the least attractive individuals; it excited love between strangers and could rekindle the flames of desire between overfamiliar lovers. British poet John Keats was well-versed in the classics, so perhaps it is no coincidence that his fatal faery woman, *La Belle Dame sans Merci*, is offered a "a garland for her head/ And bracelets too, and fragrant zone" by the man who falls under her spell. Friedrich Schiller summarised the nature of this accessory:

> "Aphrodite preserves her beauty concealed by her girdle;
> That which lends her her charms is what covers her shame."

Aphrodite in Art

After her arrival in Greece, the sculpted iconography of the goddess continued to evolve. The most ancient statutes had shown her clothed and looking severe, but she subsequently began to appear naked, perhaps rising from the sea, or else from her bath. In due course, any divine aspects of these images tended to vanish and Aphrodite became a representation of the most ideal feminine beauty, laughing, alluring and desirable: hence the Spartan temple to *Aphrodite Morpho* (the shapely).

The statue called the Knidian Aphrodite was created by the famed Praxiteles for a temple in Anatolia and was renowned as the first ever life-sized statue of a naked woman. Her right-hand hovers over her groin, a gesture of concealment and modesty that tends nonetheless to have an opposite effect for the viewer. A vogue also developed for 'wet dress' Aphrodites, in which the deity is clad in thin material that clings revealingly to her body: a good example is to be found on the so-called Ludovisi throne, an item made in Greece but removed to Rome at some point. On this, the goddess is seen rising from the sea, her transparent garment draped tightly against her skin.

Whilst many classical statues of the goddess are womanly, if not wholly matronly, Aphrodite did not necessarily lose the youthful aspect she derived from Ishtar/ Astarte. The Esquiline Venus, found on the Esquiline Hill in Rome in 1874, has distinctly juvenile breasts: small, conical, high and separate. The same is true of a bronze Venus found at St Albans and of the 'Capuan Venus,' dated to about 300BCE and now in Naples. Her plump nipples are very evidently those of a younger teenager. The Aphrodite of Soli (Soloi) on Cyprus is more striking still. The goddess in this case is envisaged in her late teens, at the peak of her physical charms and very aware of it. She stands with her head held high, challenging the viewer not to be awed by her taut flesh. She is simultaneously desirable and intimidating.

Interestingly, given the connection between the goddess and prostitution, leading courtesans were the models for several of the most famous images of Aphrodite. A very successful and rich sex worker called Phryne sat for the sculptor Praxiteles when he created the statue for a temple at Knidos. She was also the model for a painting by Apelles of the goddess emerging from the sea. The link goes further though: Phryne was given a statue of Eros by Praxiteles, who was also her lover, and she in turn presented it to the temple of Eros in her home town of Thespiai. At Lokroi Epizephyroi in southern Italy, another prostitute called Polyarchis presented the temple of Aphrodite with a wood and gold statue of the deity. Local poetess Nossis noted that the donor could afford this because her "splendid body [had] brought her wealth." Everyone would have known this, of course, both in the town *and* at the temple, so it's plain that in classical times there was no thought of temples refusing gifts funded by sex work, nor any objections to the display of images modelled on well-known sex workers.[22]

---

[22] This link between sex work and art persisted: in his 1958 poem *Santa Maria del Popolo*, Thom Gunn remarked how Caravaggio had painted a "firm insolent young whore in Venus' clothes."

ROME

The advent and expansion of the Roman Empire further helped the spread of the cult of Aphrodite. She had, of course, already travelled from Mesopotamia to the eastern Mediterranean, from which the Phoenicians had carried her worship to North Africa and to Spain, whilst Greek influence had introduced her into Sicily, Etruria and Latium. The Roman hegemony only served to consolidate her status and cult.

One reason for the continued expansion of Aphrodite's cult was that she was familiar to the Romans. They already had a fertility goddess, Venus, whose name might be traced back through the Queen, *wanassa*, on Cyprus into the deep roots of Indo-European mythology, and a temple to *Venus Obsequens*, the Indulgent Venus, stood on the Aventine Hill in Rome. A statute to Astarte captured during the wars against the Carthaginians was installed in another temple on the Capitoline. Festivals in the Venus' name took place throughout the year, with the Romans identifying several different aspects of the goddess to worship, such as *Venus Felix*, the fruitful or abundant, and *Venus Victrix*, victorious Venus.

Another aspect of the Venus' personality was inherited from Libitina, the Roman goddess of funerals. She had a shrine on the Esquiline Hill which was associated with death and burial arrangements. Originally, though, she seems to have been an earth deity concerned with the pleasures of life. This connection, and her name, led to confusion with Venus *Lubentia*, or *Lubentina*, whose title derived from the same root as *libido* and who was much more clearly a divinity of physical delight (*lubentia*).

Even better than all of this respect and adoration from the common people was the fact that the cult of Venus-Aphrodite attracted friends in high places in Rome. The clan of the Iulii claimed descent from her, through the Trojan Aeneas, and its greatest son, Julius Caesar, became one of her leading devotees. After he had been victorious in the civil war against Pompey, Caesar decided to build a huge temple in the Forum which he dedicated to *Venus Genetrix,* mother of the people, thereby emphasising the need for peace and unity in the aftermath of strife. Later, perhaps less harmoniously, Caesar set up a statue of his lover Cleopatra in the guise of the goddess in the same shrine. In Egypt, there was precedent for this, as Arsinoe II, Cleopatra's ancestor, was celebrated as *Aphrodite Euploia* (Aphrodite of the Good-Sailing), although this admittedly happened after her death – not whilst she was still a young and politically active woman.

During Roman times, too, Aphrodite merged with another goddess, Egyptian Isis, and was worshipped with her as a joint deity. Isis was the female deity of love and of fertility; she helped mothers, invented marriage, protected seafarers and raised her husband-brother from death. There were many parallels between her and Aphrodite-Astarte (indeed, the cult of Isis may even have entered Egypt from Syria, from the land of Ashtoreth), but sexuality was certainly a key element, something which is demonstrated by the statues of the goddess lifting her skirt to viewers.

DIVERSITY

Despite all of Aphrodite's affairs with male divinities and humans, it should not be assumed that her cult was felt to be strictly heterosexual. We have already seen transvestite gay priests in Mesopotamia and this tradition stayed with the goddess into the Greek and Roman periods. A number of statues have been found at sanctuaries to the goddess that depict a bearded priestess. Alternatively, the goddess herself might be represented raising her dress to reveal a penis beneath. Such images date back as far as the fifth century BCE.[23]

All the other evidence we have for the cult of Aphrodite indicates that these intersex figures are entirely to be expected. Various ancient Greek historians agreed that the goddess could take a male form, even to the extent of the deity being called Aphroditos, a masculine form of the name. For example, the Roman author Macrobius, in his *Saturnalia*, mentioned Venus as a powerful god, rather than goddess, and referred to a statue that could be seen on Cyprus, which depicted a deity with a man's beard, a woman's dress and a penis. Acts of worship to him included drinking wine, offerings of floral wreaths incorporating myrtle, and the male and female celebrants swapping their clothes and imitating the opposite sex, just as Aphrodite herself was able to appear as either male or female as she wished. Aphroditos was associated with the moon and this, combined with the dual gender, indicates clearly that s/he was a fertility deity.[24]

One of the goddess' many affairs was with Hermes and their union produced a son. He was named Hermaphroditus, after both of them, and he was a strikingly beautiful youth. A story tells that the nymph of a spring at Salmacis fell madly in love with the boy and prayed to the Olympian gods to be united with him forever. They answered, not perhaps as she had hoped, by uniting the two into one body of both sexes, a hermaphrodite. S/he then became one of the Erotes, the winged 'cupids' that formed the goddess' retinue, but there was also a minor separate cult to this intersex deity in Greece. This seems to be attested by the fact that a number of statues and figurines of Aphroditos-Hermaphroditus are known, spread right across the breadth of the former Roman Empire.[25]

---

23 For instance, at Amathus and at Golgoi, both on Cyprus.
24 Macrobius, *Saturnalia*, vol.3, book 8, para.2; Theophrastus, *Characters*, 16, 10; Philostratus, *Imagines*, 1, 2.
25 Other stories make Eros (Cupid) the child of Venus and Mars (Aphrodite and Ares).

What's more, amongst the other Erotes, several seem to have had roles presiding over same-sex desire. For example, Eros was associated with male athleticism and his statues were set up in the gymnasia where athletes trained, strongly suggesting a function as a patron of gay love. Hence the Greek poet, Meleager of Gadara, wrote:

> "The Cyprian's a woman: she pelts
> Us with insane fire for girls.
> But Eros drives our appetite to
> Males. Then which must I
>
> Lean to, his mother or her child?
> I tell you this, the Cyprian
> Will confess it's her pert child
> Who comes off always best."

The inclusion of images of the Erotes in other (non-sexual) scenes, for example images of two women together, has been interpreted as a sign that the individuals depicted should be regarded as lovers.[26]

In the temple of Astarte in Afqa, Lebanon, rites were performed as late as the fourth century CE that preserved the sanctity of diverse sexuality. Our record of this comes from Bishop Eusebius Pamphilus of Caesarea, a polemical writer who was keen to emphasise the barbarities of paganism and to celebrate their suppression, so he underscores the immorality of the goings-on at the temple, dedicated as it was to a "foul demon called Venus":

> "It was a school of godlessness for those dissipated men who had ruined their bodies in the pursuit of luxuriousness. The men were soft and effeminate; they were no longer

---

26 Rabinowitz, *Among Women,* 2001, 125–126.

men. They believed they must worship their god with impure lust. Dishonest traffic with women, secret obscene proceedings, dishonourable and indescribable things took place in the temple, where there was no law and order and no guardians to insist on good conduct."

"Their very lust and passion and impure disease of the soul, the members of the body which tempt to obscenity, and even the lack of control in shameful pleasure, they described under the titles of Cupid, Priapus, Venus, and other kindred terms."

Of course, all that these words really highlight is the gulf between Eusebius' perspective and that of the Phoenician worshippers. This incomprehension was to last for another two millennia.[27]

To conclude, historian Bettany Hughes has encapsulated the situation by saying that Aphrodite was "a divine incarnation of the many possibilities of the world. She nourished sexuality of all forms as a surging life force."[28]

SACRED SEX

Sacred, temple, cult or religious prostitution are practices that involve paid intercourse performed in the context of religious worship, possibly as a form of fertility rite or divine marriage. The terms "sacred sex" or "sacred sexual rites" are applied in those cases where payment for services is *not* involved. Such institutions are known across the world, for example under the Hittites, in ancient Israel, India, Japan and Mesoamerica. In recent decades there has been active academic debate about the existence or extent of sacred prostitution. Nevertheless, it's

---

27 Eusebius, *The Life of Constantine*, Book 3. Chapter 55; *Oration in Praise of Constantine*, c.13.
28 Hughes, *Venus & Aphrodite*, 82.

well worth noting Bettany Hughes' avowedly 'common sense' comment on this issue. She observes that, in a period when sex was seen as potentially transformational – and certainly not sinful – *and* when it was often the case that sex was a woman's only source of income, "It would perhaps be strange if both the buyer and seller had *not* wrapped the chance for sex in a religious mantle... So, sacred prostitution would be odd, not if present, but if absent."[29]

According to Herodotus, the rites performed in the temples of Mylitta around the Babylonian empire included sexual intercourse, or what scholars have later termed 'sacred sexual rites:'

> "The most shameful Babylonian custom is that which compels every woman of the land to sit in the temple of Aphrodite [by whom he means Ishtar] and have intercourse with some stranger at least once in her life. Many women who are rich and proud and disdain to mingle with the rest, drive to the temple in covered carriages drawn by teams, and stand there with a great retinue of attendants. But most sit down in the sacred precinct of Aphrodite, with their hair braided on their heads; there is a great multitude of women coming and going; passages marked by line run every way through the crowd, by which the men pass and make their choice. Once a woman has taken her place there, she may not go away to her home before some stranger has cast money into her lap, and had intercourse with her outside the temple grounds; but while he casts the money, he must say, "I invite you in the name of Mylitta". It does not matter what sum the money is; the woman will never refuse, for that would be a sin, the money being by this act made sacred. So, she follows the first man who casts it and rejects no one. After their intercourse, having discharged

---

29 Hughes, *Venus & Aphrodite*, 68–69.

her sacred duty to the goddess, she goes away to her home; and thereafter there is no bribe however great that will get her to have sex again. Naturally, the women that are fairest and tallest are soon free to depart, but the less comely have long to wait because they cannot fulfil the law; for some of them remain for three years, or four. There is a custom like this in some parts of Cyprus."[30]

Herodotus feigns shock and revulsion, but it's still a spicy story that's too good to miss out. Despite being Greek, he seems reluctant to admit that similar practices actually prevailed within his own culture, and he fails to appreciate that the women involved were not regarded as loose and unfaithful, but that their presence at the temple meant that they were transformed into priestesses, or servants of the goddess, and as such were approached in a reverent manner.

It is believed that sacred sexual services, offered by both males and females, were a custom of the ancient Phoenicians. These were performed in honour of the deities Astarte and Adonis as part of festivals in the cities of Byblos, Afqa and Baalbek and in the Syrian city of Palmyra. Both paid and unpaid sex was available. Those prostituting for pay did so as an act of worship to the deity, their earnings being devoted to the temple. In addition, every virgin had to honour the goddess by presenting herself for sex seven days in succession at Astarte's temple – but in fact both married women and their single daughters are said to have honoured Astarte with their bodies.

The Etruscan site of Pyrgi, on the Tyrrhenian coast in central Italy, was another centre for the worship of Astarte. Here, archaeologists have identified a temple consecrated to her and built with at least seventeen small rooms annexed that may very well have served as quarters for the temple's famous sacred prostitutes. Similarly, a temple dedicated to Atargatis (a Syrian

---

30 Herodotus, *Histories*.

goddess who was identified with Aphrodite) in Dura-Europos, on the Euphrates, was found to have a dozen similar small rooms with low benches, which might have been intended for sex. Archaeological records also provide evidence of religious prostitution in Lydia (Turkey) and in Armenia, where noble families would present their unmarried daughters at the temple of Anaitis (or Anahida), a local deity who was equated with Ishtar/Aphrodite. Greek geographer Strabo recorded as well that "the Egyptians consecrate to Zeus [i.e. Amun] one of the most beautiful girls born of an illustrious family. She becomes a prostitute and has relations with whoever she chooses until the moment of purification of her body takes place [i.e her first menstruation]. After this, she is given in marriage to a man, but before this a ceremony of mourning for her period of divine prostitution will be held in her honour."[31]

In Carthage in North Africa, sacred sex was associated to the city of Sicca, which the Romans called Sicca Veneria because of its temple of Astarte or Tanit (Roman Venus). Roman writer Valerius Maximus described how women engaged in prostitution with visitors in return for gifts which were then put towards their eventual dowries. Several temples to Astarte in Carthaginian Spain also seem to have featured sacred prostitutes, notably at Cadiz, which was renowned for its erotic dancers, termed *puellae gaditanae* (Gadiz girls) in Latin.

As we already know, a major centre of the cult of Astarte-Aphrodite was Cyprus, the main temples being located in Paphos, Amathus and Kition. Inscriptions from the latter record personal economic activity taking place in the temple, for any earnings derived from sacred prostitution would have been taxed by the state just like the income of any other businesses. We do know that the Cypriot custom was for all women, before they married, to offer themselves for sex with strangers at the

---

31 Strabo, *Geographika*, Book XVII, c.1, para.46.

sanctuaries of the goddess. James Frazer explained that "the practice was clearly regarded not as an orgy of lust, but as a solemn religious duty performed in the service of [the Great Mother Goddess.]"[32]

Meanwhile, it was alleged that religious prostitution at Paphos had been instituted by King Cinyras, who devoted his daughters to sexual service of the goddess. This particular monarch is surrounded by myths. His son Adonis, who was to become Aphrodite's lover, was conceived through an incestuous relationship between Cinyras and his own mother. The king himself was also pursued by the goddess whilst his father-in-law was the well-known Pygmalion, a Phoenician king of Cyprus who notoriously fell in love with a statute of Aphrodite. What we seem to have here is a garbled memory of a rite in which the king symbolically married the goddess, Astarte, and then (as in Sumer) had sex with either the high priestess or one of the temple prostitutes, who would have been acting the role of the divinity.[33]

Furthermore, the Greek geographer Strabo recorded that on Cyprus, near the mountain peak called Olympus, there was "a temple of Aphrodite Acraea, which cannot be entered or seen by women." The author doesn't expand upon what he means by this, but it's possible to suggest an explanation. 'Acraea' simply signifies that the shrine was on a hill – as was often the case, Corinth being another example. It would, though, seem very odd if all females had been permanently excluded from the temple of a goddess so intimately concerned with their affairs, so we may deduce that what Strabo meant was that married or sexually active women couldn't enter. However, as young virgins, they would have made the pilgrimage to the mountain top to offer themselves for Aphrodite.[34]

---

32 Frazer, *Golden Bough*, c.31.
33 Frazer, *Golden Bough*, c.31.
34 Strabo, *Geographika*, XIV, 6.

The practice of holy harlotry was also known on the mainland of classical Greece. Around the year 2 BC, Strabo, in his description of the town of Corinth, recorded some of the practices of female temple servants in the temple of Aphrodite there, although these may relate to some centuries earlier:

> "The temple of Aphrodite was so rich that it employed more than a thousand *hetairae* [high class prostitutes] whom both men and women had given to the goddess. Many people visited the town on account of them, and thus these *hetairae* contributed to the riches of the place: for the ship captains frivolously spent their money there, hence the saying: 'The voyage to Corinth is not for every man'."[35]

He then recounted the story of a *hetaira* being reproached for not undertaking manual work and responding with a boast about the money she made. Elsewhere in the same text, Strabo referred to the "women earning money with their bodies" at the shrine, whereas the author Athenaeus rather more poetically described being "in the lovely beds picking the fruits of the mildest bloom" when discussing the delights of a visit to the Corinthian temple.[36]

In 464 BC, a Corinthian called Xenophon dedicated one hundred young girls to the temple of the goddess in thanks for his success at the Olympian games. The Theban poet Pindar was commissioned to write a hymn celebrating the donation of these girls, who would thereafter 'graze' in the Cyprian's grove. He went on:

> "You girls who make so many guests welcome,
> As servants of Peitho in sumptuous Corinth;
> Who burn yellow incense whilst, again
> And again, you send your thoughts flying

---
35 *Geographika*, VIII, 6, 20.
36 *Geographika*, XII, 3, 36; Athenaeus, *The Deipnosophists*, XIII, 574.

Up to Erotes' mother;
Aphrodite of Heaven –

Children, she has granted you this, that
Without blame you harvest the fruit of your
Tender season on the beds of desire. Such a duty
Is wholly beautiful..."[37]

These various examples indicate how the sexualised cult of Aphrodite spread from Cyprus across the whole of the Greek-influenced and colonised parts of the Mediterranean. As a result, sacred prostitution was known as far apart as Sicily and in the Pontus (in the temple of Enyo or Ma at Comana) – where Strabo alleged there to have been six thousand prostitutes, both male and female, at a single temple site.[38]

As we have already seen in respect of artworks, there was a two-way traffic between the goddess and the prostitutes. They gave pleasure in honour of Aphrodite and they reflected this in their relationship with her. An epigram by the Greek poet Nikarchos describes a girl who decides to become a courtesan, promising the 'Cyprian' ten per cent of all her earnings if she meets with success in her new career. As protector of working girls, Venus was specially honoured by them in Rome at the festival of Vinalia. Ovid advised:

"You common wenches, celebrate the divinity of Venus: Venus favours the earnings of ladies of a liberal profession. Offer incense and pray for beauty and popular favour; pray to be charming and witty; give to the Queen her own myrtle and the mint she loves, and bands or rushes hidden in clustered roses."[39]

---

37 Pindar, fragment 122S, cited in Chamaeleon, *On Pindar*, Athen. 13.573B–574B.
38 Strabo, *Geographika*, XII, 2, 3.
39 Ovid, *Fasti*, April 23rd.

Another Greeks title for the divinity was *Aphrodite Pandemos* (also known as *Venus vulgivaga*) – the people's goddess, the common Aphrodite – and, in this guise, she was the especial patron of whores and rent boys. The statue of this goddess in Athens was funded jointly by all the hetaerae of the city.

We also have poems about retiring prostitutes, who presented the local temple of the goddess with the 'tools of their trade' (mirror, comb, girdle and jewellery). Leonidas of Tarentum described how one woman called Kallikleia thanked Aphrodite for having granted her wishes by hanging up, in the porch of the shrine, a silver anklet, "the purple curls of her Lesbian hair, her translucent bra." Another such, a fifty-year-old called Nicias, gave the goddess items that included her sandals and "the things of which a man may not speak."[40]

We might speculate whether these unmentionable items were, in fact, various sex toys for customers. As we'll see later, Pierre Louys imagined in his *Chansons de Bilitis* how a woman might visit a lesbian acquaintance to borrow an "object" to take with her when she visits her young girlfriend Myrrhina – 'So little, so pretty, so lascivious.' Bilitis can't assist with the request and directs the caller to the local leather worker. In Herondas' mime, *The Gossiping Friends*, a very similar scene takes place, with a visitor asking to see her host's '*baubo.*' She's informed that these items are made by the local cobbler Kerdo – and "When I saw them, my eyes nearly burst out with desire. The men certainly have no rams like those! ... their smoothness – a dream; and the stitches – of down, not of thread! Hunt as you might, you could not find another cobbler so kindly disposed toward women." Baubo is the name of a woman who is said to have cheered up the goddess Demeter with 'something' she had under her skirt. That special something seems to have been an *olisbos* – literally, a 'slider.' In Aristophanes' comedy, *Lysistrata*,

---

[40] Philitas of Samos, *Anthologia Graeca*, vol.6, 285, 210 & 211.

the heroine bewails the absence of the men at war, and complains how: "I have not once seen even an eight-inch *olisbos* as a leather consolation for us poor widows." Once again, we are reminded by this evidence that any and all pleasures were sacred to Aphrodite – and that she would not have objected in the least to Nicias dedicating her dildo at her shrine.[41]

The sight of the sacred prostitutes waiting for customers in the temples must have been a very familiar sight around the shrines of Aphrodite and Astarte. We know this for a fact because we have a number of images of girls at windows discovered at ancient sites: the Metropolitan Museum of Art in New York has three Assyrian examples; the Louvre has a terracotta plaque found at Idalion on Cyprus.[42]

Another link between Aphrodite and working girls was *kosmesis* – adornment. As we've just seen with the donations of mirrors and hairpieces, prostitutes linked the act of getting made up and dressed up with the love goddess – and there was good reason for this. In many ancient sources Aphrodite is depicted applying perfume, doing her hair and putting on see-through clothes so as to make herself more attractive. The scents of myrrh, cinnamon, clove, cassia and fennel were especially hers; the mirror is one of her symbols, very familiar indeed to us today as the female symbol of a circle with a cross handle.[43]

For a long time, members of the new Christian cult within the empire had railed against the worship of Aphrodite. The theologian Clement of Alexandria (150–215) was especially vocal in his attacks on the "wanton serving wench" and her "lewd orgies." As for the cult's idea of physical love as a form of holy communion:

---

41 Louys, *Bilitis*, song 75; Herondas, *Sixth Mime*; Aristophanes, *Lysistrata*, verses 108–110.
42 *Greek Anthology*, poems 46 & 88.
43 See for example the fifth *Homeric Hymn*, to Aphrodite, in which she prepares to seduce Anchises (lines 53–74).

"This is an insult to the name of communion ... communion is good when the word refers to sharing of money and food and clothing ... These thrice wretched men treat carnal and sexual intercourse as a sacred religious mystery, and think that it will bring them to the kingdom of God ... It is to the brothels that this 'communion' leads. They can have pigs and goats as their associates. Those who have most to hope from them are the public harlots who shamelessly receive all who want to come to them."

Later, Clement expressed the viewpoint that set Christianity so much at odds with the worship of Aphrodite:

"I agree with Antisthenes when he says, 'Could I catch Aphrodite, I would shoot her; for she has destroyed many of our beautiful and good women.' And he says that 'Love is a vice of nature, and the wretches who fall under its power call the disease a deity.' For in these words, it is shown that stupid people are overcome through ignorance with pleasure, to which we ought to give no admittance, even though it be called a god, that is, though it be given by God for the necessity of procreation."[44]

As a final comment, Clement noted how statutes of Aphrodite had been modelled on Phryne and asked his readers contemptuously: "It remains for you to judge whether you ought to worship courtesans." This was a rhetorical question, with only one correct answer...

The emperor Constantine, after his conversion to Christianity in 313, closed down a number of temples to Venus or similar deities in Rome, as well as stamping out temple prostitution in the Phoenician cities of Afqa and Heliopolis (Baalbek) in Lebanon. The destruction of the latter site was praised by Bishop Eusebius as one of the emperor's noblest acts, for it had formerly

---

[44] Clement, 'Exhortations to the Heathens,' *Stromata*, Book 3, chapter 4; Book 2, c.20.

been a shrine where "those, who dignify licentious pleasure with a distinguishing title of honour, had permitted their wives and daughters to commit shameless fornication."[45]

Whilst the extent of *sacred* prostitution may be disputed, there is no doubt that Aphrodite was felt to have a special links not only to sex but to sex workers. So strong were these that Roman writer Ennius, translating the Greek Euhemerus, alleged that Venus was originally an ordinary woman who had invented prostitution and had then been elevated to divinity (a perfect example of the process of 'euhemerising'). The key point, though, is this: however, and with whomsoever, you did it, was perfectly irrelevant to the goddess: pleasure was her only concern.

ECSTASY

Aphrodite's cult had links with those of Dionysos-Bacchus. The goddess is said to have been the lover of Dionysos, who was another deity of fertility. The festival held in the latter's honour included a procession which symbolised the return of Spring, just as happened at Aphrodite's shrines.[46]

Ecstatic rites were part of the worship of both divinities, as well as of the rites of related gods such as Cybele, Attis, Isis and Sabazios. Dionysus' ceremonies, the 'bacchanals,' were attended by delirious female participants called, variously, *maenads, bassarids, bacchae, bacchantes, thyiades, lenae, clodones* and *mimallones*. All the names denote the women's frantic state as they danced wildly, dressed in animal skins and engaged in ecstatic orgies. In 1886 Austrian painter Gustav Klimt painted a memorable image of the *Altar of Dionysus* for a staircase in the *Burgtheater* in Vienna, in which two naked adolescent girls, identified as maenads, appear before the god's shrine. One reclines, seemingly exhausted by the orgy, and languidly holds

---

45 Eusebius, *The Life of Constantine*, Book 3. Chapter 58.
46 B. Hughes, *Venus & Aphrodite*, 54.

up some flowers; the other presents a statue. To one side a satyr figure plays on a drum and in the background lurk two young children with strangely black eyes (their pupils hugely expanded by drugs perhaps?).

APHRODITE & MARY

As previously mentioned, the Christianisation of the Roman Empire spelled the end of officially sanctioned worship of Aphrodite-Venus. Even so, it's worth observing that the level of invective directed against the love goddess by the church fathers only goes to show how strong devotion to her remained, several centuries into the Christian era. Eventually though, her temples ceased to be used and were widely destroyed, quite commonly by building churches on top of them – a regular practice of the early Church. Many of the pagan gods were rebranded as saints, too, hence we have St. Venera (Venus) as well as Saints Artemidos (Artemis), Mercourios (Mercury) and Dionysius (Dionysos). On Cyprus, at the site of the temple at Paphos, a church was built dedicated to the Blessed Aphroditissa.

Despite this suppression, however, the goddess of love did not vanish and was not forgotten. As Geoffrey Grigson said, this was because of a very simple, human fact: that she "stood for something too important in our nature to disappear." Many of her attributes were inherited by the Virgin Mary; Bettany Hughes has summarised the identity between them very well: "In many ways, particularly in the East, Mary of Nazareth was the ancient, teenage mother goddess." Mary had a famous belt, just like Aphrodite; the dove was her messenger at the Annunciation; she is frequently seen in celestial form with a halo of stars and she is, of course, approached by supplicants for her maternal, caring qualities, the Christian all-mother as well as the mother of God.[47]

---

47 Grigson, *The Goddess of Love*, 229.

Conceptions of the ancient love goddess didn't vanish entirely, though. Memories of her as the patron of love and lovers remained, the subject of poetic reference, thereby sustaining her power long enough for it to be revived in the European Renaissance. In England, Geoffrey Chaucer and John Lydgate wrote about her. More remarkably, perhaps, Dante incorporated her into his *Divine Comedy*. In the *Purgatory* he alluded both to Venus and to Cupid, her "wayward child;" in the *Paradise*, he described how "the fair Cyprian... shed love's madness on the yet un-ransomed world."[48]

The recovery of Greek and Roman civilisation that occurred in Italy from the mid-fifteenth century onwards restored to us much of the ancient mythology. Stories of Venus, along with those of the other gods and goddesses, became the common currency of educated people and scenes from these became familiar subjects for artists and their clients. The Humanist Angelo Poliziano translated and published Hesiod and the *Homeric Hymn* to Aphrodite and restored to us the story of her oceanic birth. Sandro Botticelli read this work and then painted his *Birth of Venus*. Subsequent translations made the stories of Venus and Adonis, the judgment of Paris, and the travails of Aphrodite, Mars and Vulcan, just as much the common currency of cultured Europe as the legend of the divine birth and they have featured again and again on canvases and in sculptures ever since.

The goddess was not lost in popular culture either. Sailors used to have a star tattooed on their hands in her honour, hoping that she would steer them home safely from the sea. It need hardly be added that Venus remains to this day the divine bringer of love, celebrated across the entire world on Valentine's Day with offerings of her red roses at the temple of love.

---

48 Chaucer, *House of Fame;* Lydgate, *Troy Book;* Dante, *Purgatorio*, XXVIII, 65 & *Paradiso*, VIII, 1–3.

Odes to Aphrodite – Poetry

Given humankind's obsession with matters of finding and losing lovers, poems to the goddess of love are the stock-in-trade of Western literature and, as such, they are not always the greatest works. Nonetheless, the sheer bulk of verse produced testifies to – as well as perpetuating – the position of Venus. Most of the vicissitudes of love were set out by poets in classical Greece, at the dawn of Aphrodite's reign, and little that is truly new has been said since.

SAPPHO

The Greek poet Sappho wrote a considerable number of poems invoking and addressing Aphrodite, seeking her aid in times of trouble. She described herself as a devoted slave to the goddess, her "Peerless Mistress," and implored her to intervene in matters of love.[1]

In Sappho's verse, Aphrodite could be portrayed the cause of the poet's woes, as in *Blame Aphrodite:*

> "It's no use Mother dear,
> I can't finish my weaving
> You may blame Aphrodite
>
> Soft as she is
> She has almost killed me
> With love for that boy."

---
1 *Aphrodite's Doves.*

When affairs of the heart went well, the goddess was celebrated and adored by contented lovers, but she was probably invoked most frequently when there was yearning or loss.

> "I have had not one word from her.
> Frankly I wish I were dead.
> When she left, she wept
>
> a great deal; she said to
> me, 'This parting must be
> endured, Sappho. I go unwillingly.'
>
> I said, 'Go, and be happy
> but remember (you know
> well) whom you leave shackled by love.'
>
> 'If you forget me, think
> of our gifts to Aphrodite
> and all the loveliness that we shared –'
>
> 'All the violet tiaras,
> braided rosebuds, dill and
> crocus twined around your young neck,'
>
> 'Myrrh poured on your head
> And, on soft mats, girls, with
> all that they most wished for beside them,'
>
> 'While no voices chanted
> choruses without ours,
> no woodlot bloomed in spring without song..."

Alternatively, Aphrodite might be asked to intervene when affairs of the heart did not run to plan, as in Sappho's *Ode* to the goddess, in which she sought relief from the pain of an unrequited love – and was answered:

> "She that fain would fly, she shall quickly follow,
> She that now rejects, yet with gifts shall woo thee,
> She that heeds thee not, soon shall love to madness,
> Love thee, the loth one!"

All this will happen, Sappho tells the deity, if "you yourself join forces on my side!"

So far, the emphasis has been on Aphrodite as the ultimate source of joy, bringing couples together and making their dreams real. Of course, even with the highs of love there can be lows; Sappho knew this, as did Greek dramatist Euripides, who in *Hippolytos* has the doomed Phaedra's nurse declare:

> "If the Cyprian falls on us, it's no good
> Resisting. If we yield, she will come on us
> Gently. If she finds us disdainful, she will
> Abuse us – oh, you can't think how severely...
> It is she who sows and gives love – by
> Which all of us on the earth have our being."

Sappho and her contemporaries established many of the basic themes of poems to Venus, emphasising especially the pain and pleasure that love can bring. Few subsequent authors have strayed far from this template. Over and above that, Sappho could openly address the goddess about the girls she longed for: as poet Geoffrey Grigson observed, the poetess, "the Greeks, and Aphrodite as well, knew more ... about the kinds and inclusiveness of sex, and were honest about it [more than many later, prudish writers]."[2]

---

2 Grigson, *The Goddess of Love*, 109.

ROBERT HERRICK

A number of sixteenth and seventeenth century British poets made use of the legends of Venus-Aphrodite, John Fletcher and William Shakespeare included, but as a stepping stone to more modern verse I shall consider Robert Herrick, an Anglican vicar whose poetry in many respects contradicts the staid image we might form of him. Whereas we might not be surprised when Fletcher described Venus as the "mother of delights/Crowner of all happy nights," similar sentiments from a churchman can seem unexpected and out of character.[3]

Herrick certainly wrote some conventional love poems, invoking romantic Venus,[4] but he also said of his 1648 collection, *Hesperides*, that it included "cleanly-Wantonesse." It is indeed the case that he was openly appreciative of female physical charms in a manner that can be very startling to us today, but which he would surely have felt to be perfectly natural and healthy (as, for that matter, would Venus). It follows from this that his treatment of the goddess is equally frank, as we see in *How Lillies came white*:

> "White though ye be; yet, Lillies, know,
> From the first ye were not so;
> But I'll tell ye
> What befell ye:
> Cupid and his Mother lay
> In a cloud, while both did play,
> He with his pretty finger press'd
> The rubie niplet of her breast;
> Out of which the cream of light,

---

3 Fletcher, *To Venus*.
4 See, for example, *A Hymn to Cupid or A Vow to Venus*; likewise, girls at Miss Portman's school in Putney were compared to "sixty Venuses, or ... fairies, syrens, nymphs" (*The School, or Pearl, of Putney*). There are, too, numerous poems involving Cupid.

> Like to a dew,
> Fell down on you
> And made ye white."

This image may very well remind us of Bronzino's incestuous *Allegory of Lust,* which will be described later. Herrick's Venus is undoubtedly carnal and very human in her emotions, which his verse *How Violets came blew* demonstrates well:

> "Love on a day, wise poets tell,
> Some time in wrangling spent,
> Whether the violets should excel,
> Or she, in sweetest scent.
>
> But Venus having lost the day,
> Poor girls, she fell on you:
> And beat ye so, as some dare say,
> Her blows did make ye blew."

Herrick often praised his loved-ones' breasts and nipples. His *Description of a Woman* is one example that, instead of alluding to strawberries and cream, uses the classics to this end:

> "Her breast, a place for beauty's throne most fit,
> Bears up two globes where love and pleasure sit,
> Which, headed with two rich, round rubies, show
> Like wanton rosebuds growing out of snow;
> And in the milky valley that's between
> Sits Cupid, kissing of his mother queen,
> Fingering the paps that feel like sieved silk,
> And press'd a little they will weep pure milk."

In a short ode *To Dianeme* Herrick went even further, complimenting his lady's legs, her thighs, her "fleshie principalities ... that Hill (where smiling Love doth sit)/Having a living fountain under it." This metaphor recalls the Greek and Roman jokes about 'Aphrodite's smile' and underlines how much she remained the deity of physical love. Another classical reference is found in the poet's lines *Upon Julia's Riband*; tied around her waist, it is "that Zonulet of love/Wherein all pleasures of the world are wove." The same girdle is mentioned in Herrick's *Epithalamion to Sir Thomas Southwell and His Lady;* the young couple were newly married and Herrick called on the goddess for her assistance: "O Venus! thou to whom is known/The best way how to loose the zone/Of virgins."

A Nuptial Song, or Epithalamy on Sir Clipseby Crew and his Lady was composed for another marriage. In the verse Herrick demonstrated familiarity with all the key facets of Aphrodite's cult: the bride is likened to the goddess, born from the sea, wrapped in transparent fabrics, and advancing onto the land in a shower of rose petals, "spicing the chaft air with fumes of Paradise" (pomegranates and cinnamon) as she brings Spring with her to the countryside.[5]

In *A Short Hymn to Venus*, Herrick even petitions the help of the goddess for himself:

> "Goddess, I do love a girl,
> Ruby-lipp'd and tooth'd with pearl;
> If so be I may but prove
> Lucky in this maid I love,
> I will promise there shall be
> Myrtles offer'd up to thee."

Similarly, in the *Hymn to Venus and Cupid*, Herrick deployed his knowledge of the classical myths alongside a frank appreciation of the carnal delights of a conjugal love:

> "Sea-born goddess, let me be
> By thy son thus grac'd and thee;
> That whene'er I woo, I find

---

[5] See too Herrick's mentions of honey, myrtle and doves in *The Bag of the Bee*.

> Virgins coy but not unkind.
> Let me, when I kiss a maid,
> Taste her lips so overlaid
> With love's syrup, that I may,
> In your temple when I pray,
> Kiss the altar and confess
> There's in love no bitterness."

We shall encounter these honeyed lips again later, albeit in a very different context.

NINETEENTH CENTURY VERSE

Victorian views of the goddess in her different guises varied quite considerably. The Australian poet Henry Kendall (1839–1882) wrote a poem titled *Astarte* which is a lament to a long-lost, deceased love, who never knew his passion. The goddess is aware of the poet's yearning for his "Dead Love's wild Nevermore!" – and his wish to be free of the memory – and she shares his grief and pain:

> "Astarte, Syrian sister,
> Your face is wet with tears;
> I think you know the secret
> One heart hath held for years!"

Unlike Sappho's deity, Astarte cannot help, but she can empathise. For the French poet Paul Armand Silvestre (1837–1901), though, *Astarte* is a cruel mistress. She is "the relentless daughter of the wave/The immortal Beauty who tortures the world." She oversees our pain as well as our "fertile pleasures" and, being born of the sea, she has "kept for our tears the salt of the bitter flood."

American physician and poet, Oliver Wendell Holmes Senior (1809–1894), knew too the mixed benefits of love and reviewed them sardonically in his flippant (and now rather racist and misogynist) poem *The First Fan*, written in 1877. He describes the Olympians having been displaced by the 'Wandering Jew,' in other words the new cult of Jesus of Nazareth. In turn, the departing divinities offer to sell their successor their best-known possessions, such as Venus' girdle:

> "When rose the cry 'Great Pan is dead!'
> And Jove's high palace closed its portal,
> The fallen gods, before they fled,
> Sold out their frippery to a mortal…
>
> So none at last was left behind
> Save Venus, the celestial charmer.
>
> Poor Venus! What had she to sell?
> For all she looked so fresh and jaunty,
> Her wardrobe, as I blush to tell,
> Already seemed but quite too scanty.
>
> Her gems were sold, her sandals gone,
> She always would be rash and flighty,
> Her winter garments all in pawn,
> Alas for charming Aphrodite.
>
> The lady of a thousand loves,
> The darling of the old religion,
> Had only left of all the doves
> That drew her car one fan-tailed pigeon.
>
> How oft, upon her fingertips,
> He perched, afraid of Cupid's arrow,
> Or kissed her on the rosebud lips,
> Like Roman Lesbia's loving sparrow!…
>
> 'A lover's heart it quickly cools;
> In mine it kindles up enough rage

To wring their necks. How can such fools
Ask men to vote for woman suffrage?'

The goddess spoke, and gently stripped
Her bird of every caudal feather;
A strand of gold-bright hair she clipped,
And bound the glossy plumes together,

And lo, the Fan! for beauty's hand,
The lovely queen of beauty made it...

Jove, Juno, Venus, where are you?
Mars, Mercury, Phoebus, Neptune, Saturn?
But o'er the world the Wandering Jew
Has borne the Fan's celestial pattern...

And since from Aphrodite's dove
The pattern of the fan was given,
No wonder that it breathes of love
And wafts the perfumed gales of heaven!

Before this new Pandora's gift
In slavery woman's tyrant kept her,
But now he kneels her glove to lift,
The fan is mightier than the sceptre.

The tap it gives how arch and sly!
The breath it wakes how fresh and grateful!
Behind its shield how soft the sigh!
The whispered tale of shame how fateful!

Its empire shadows every throne
And every shore that man is tossed on;
It rules the lords of every zone,
Nay, even the bluest blood of Boston!

But every one that swings to-night,
Of fairest shape, from farthest region,

> May trace its pedigree aright
> To Aphrodite's fan-tailed pigeon."

Ironically, Christian culture has spread with it the cult of the love-goddess, albeit it in degraded form, and the concept of romantic monogamous love remains both an aspiration and a burden for people across the world.

Then again, for Victor James Daley (1858–1905), *Aphrodite* remained the classical beauty, awakening the world with love. She arises like a "Flower of Time" out of the waves, bringing burgeoning life to the natural world and happiness to human hearts:

> "Softly she smiled upon Man forlorn,
> And the music of love in his wild heartbeat,
> And down to the pit went his gods of gloom,
> And earth grew bright and fair as a bride,
> And folk in star-worlds wondering cried –
> 'Lo in the skies a new star is born!'"

Scottish-Australian poet James Lister Cuthbertson (1851–1910) shared a similar vision of Aphrodite in *Wattle and Myrtle*, a poem imbued with symbols from the ancient mythology:

> "Gold of the tangled wilderness of wattle,
> Break in the lone green hollows of the hills,
> Flame on the iron headlands of the ocean,
> Gleam on the margin of the hurrying rills.
>
> Come with thy saffron diadem and scatter
> Odours of Araby that haunt the air,
> Queen of our woodland, rival of the roses,
> Spring in the yellow tresses of thy hair.

Surely the old gods, dwellers on Olympus,
Under thy shining loveliness have strayed,
Crowned with thy clusters, magical Apollo,
Pan with his reedy music may have played.

Surely within thy fastness, Aphrodite,
She of the sea-ways, fallen from above,
Wandered beneath thy canopy of blossom,
Nothing disdainful of a mortal's love.

Aye, and her sweet breath lingers on the wattle,
Aye, and her myrtle dominates the glade,
And with a deep and perilous enchantment
Melts in the heart of lover and of maid."

French poet Paul Armand Silvestre (1837–1901) understood how Venus had, in fact, become an almost impossible ideal of beauty, as his poem *Venus de Milo* shows:

"It was neither living flesh nor clay
Which served as a model for this radiant body:
The woman has less pride, the earth is too fragile,
And this immortal marble comes from the land of the Gods."

For the Belgian Charles van Lerberghe, too, *Venus* was female perfection, a harbinger of love, "nude and blonde, sparkling, roseate." She comes to a sleeping woman with a "sudden flight of doves" and an entourage of "lovely nymphs" who wear "purple girdles/Beneath their breasts and Roses in their hair." The sleeper awakes in wonder and, in tears and a hushed voice, tells the goddess her bliss and her afflictions. Then, her prayers are answered:

> "And all at once...
> Through the air reeling with song and with roses,
> She, who with her breath quickens all things,
> Gently approached me...
> And I felt upon my throbbing heart all on fire
> Something like the alighting of lips."

Van Lerberghe's Venus is a very conventional and delicately feminine – but perhaps rather colourless – goddess. Many poets of the period wanted to insist on a romantically feminine goddess and shied away in horror from her active sexuality.

DANTE GABRIEL ROSSETTI

Pre-Raphaelite painter and poet Rossetti was fascinated with *femme fatale* women, lovers and goddesses, and he worked with the mythology of the goddess of love several times, most memorably in *Astarte Syriaca:*

> "Mystery: lo! betwixt the sun and moon
> Astarte of the Syrians: Venus Queen
> Ere Aphrodite was. In silver sheen
> Her twofold girdle clasps the infinite boon
> Of bliss whereof the heaven and earth commune:
> And from her neck's inclining flower-stem lean
> Love-freighted lips and absolute eyes that wean
> The pulse of hearts to the spheres' dominant tune.
> Torch-bearing, her sweet ministers compel
> All thrones of light beyond the sky and sea
> The witnesses of Beauty's face to be:
> That face, of Love's all-penetrative spell
> Amulet, talisman, and oracle –
> Betwixt the sun and moon a mystery."

This sonnet was written by Rossetti to accompany his painting of the same name. It was first published in 1877 as part of F.G. Stephens' description of the painting in the *Athenaeum*. The verse emphasises the inscrutable power of the love goddess, a vision of woman found in much of Rossetti's work. The picture shows a red-haired Astarte dressed in a dark green robe, with two identical attendants who hold torches. She adopts the 'Venus pudica' or *pudica* pose, in which her left hand covers her groin area. This is frequently seen in nude representations of the goddess – or of any naked female. The classical precedent is the statue called the Aphrodite of Knidos, carved by Praxiteles in the fourth century BCE. Other ancient statues, such as the Capitoline Venus, copied the gesture, as did much later paintings such as Giorgione's *Sleeping Venus* or Titian's *Venus of Urbino*. The pose might be meant to conceal the groin, but of course it only serves to attract attention to the goddess' most important area.

Dante Gabriel also wrote *Venus Victrix*, describing the judgment of Paris between Juno, Pallas Athena and Aphrodite. Paris chooses the latter, the "heavenly fair" sovereign, smiling inspirer of "love's tumultuous trance." Christina Rossetti, the painter-poet's sister, also wrote on the theme of the goddess, in *Venus Looking Glass*. Here, she is again envisaged as a seasonal deity of budding and fruitfulness. She is the bringer of Spring, "Around whose head white doves rose, wheeling high/ Or low, and cooed after their tender sort." The lovely "Queen of Love" then vanishes for the summer, but returns in autumn, to walk amid the wheat, bringing hope and contentment to humankind.

Æ (WILLIAM RUSSELL)

The visionary Irish poet, Russell (1867–1935), was usually concerned with the spiritual beings of Theosophy and of ancient Irish myth. His *Aphrodite* of 1913 combines these interests with classical gods:

"Not unremembering, we pass our exile from the starry ways:
One timeless hour in time we caught from the long night of endless days.
With solemn gaiety the stars danced far withdrawn on elfin heights:
The lilac breathed amid the shade of green and blue and citron lights.
But yet the close enfolding night seemed on the phantom verge of things,
For our adoring hearts had turned within from all their wanderings:
For beauty called to beauty, and there thronged at the enchanter's will
The vanished hours of love that burn within the Ever-living still.
And sweet eternal faces put the shadows of the earth to rout,
And faint and fragile as a moth your white hand fluttered and went out.
Oh, who am I who tower beside this goddess of the twilight air?
The burning doves fly from my heart, and melt within her bosom there.
I know the sacrifice of old they offered to the mighty queen,
And this adoring love has brought us back the beauty that has been.
As to her worshippers she came descending from her glowing skies,
So, Aphrodite I have seen with shining eyes look through your eyes:
One gleam of the ancestral face which lighted up the dawn for me:
One fiery visitation of the love the gods desire in thee!"

In Russell's poem, the Greek deity is transformed into a new age goddess for a revived paganism. She is a symbol of a paradise to be regained, after centuries of exile, by a people who have reconnected themselves to the spirits of nature, to the elves as well as to the Olympian gods.

ARTHUR RIMBAUD

In *Venus Anadyomene,* French Symbolist poet Rimbaud (1854–91) offers us a bleakly realistic vision of the goddess:

> "As if from a green tin coffin, a woman's head
> Rises from an old bathtub, slow and dumb,
> Hair greased back to hide bald patches
> And not succeeding very well;
>
> First: a fat grey neck, jutting shoulder blades,
> A squat back with all kinds of curves;
> Then: her heavy hips begin and never seem to end;
> Folds of fat shift beneath her skin.
>
> Her spine's a little raw, and the whole mass
> Reeks; above all, you notice irregularities
> Better appreciated under a microscope…
>
> Two words are engraved across her arse: *Clara Venus*;
> And then her body shifts and offers up her ample rump
> For a view: a repellent frame for the ulcer on her anus."[6]

Rimbaud's Venus is not some imaginary goddess, but a real, middle-aged woman, with coarse skin and an imperfect body. I assume that she's a prostitute, the tattoo on her buttocks intended to be read by clients as they bugger her, despising Clara at the same time as they make use of her. It is very likely,

---
6 translation by Wyatt Mason.

too, that this 'ulcer' is the chancre of syphilis, compounding the tragic seediness of the scene.

This Venus, for all her unsexy fleshliness and gritty, grubby reality, still has a connection with the ancient cult. As a prostitute, she is continuing in a sacred tradition and, in offering clients a range of services, she reminds us that all sexual activity is pleasing to the goddess.

Rimbaud's emphasis on backsides might seem unsuitable and unclassical, but consider the *Venus Callipyge*. This statue, the 'Venus (or Aphrodite) of the beautiful buttocks,' is a Roman marble statue, possibly a copy of an older Greek original, which is dated to around the late first century BCE. The goddess is partially clothed and is seen in the process of raising her light dress to uncover her hips and buttocks, whilst looking back and down over her shoulder, perhaps to admire and evaluate herself.

In fact, this statue's pose as we see it now is the creation of its sixteenth century restorer. It may lack historical authenticity, but very possibly it was inspired by a story recorded by the Greek rhetorician Athenaeus. He explained the origin of the temple of Aphrodite Kallipygos in Syracuse, Sicily, as being the result of a dispute between two sisters over which of them had the shapelier buttocks. They accosted a young man passing by their home to have him perform a sort of judgment of Paris. He chose the older sister. Subsequently, he developed a passion for her, which led to his younger brother going to see the girls for himself and falling in love with the younger of the pair. The two brothers married the two sisters and, as they had both become wealthy women, the girls dedicated a temple to Aphrodite, calling her *Kallipygos*. Various later copies of the restored statue have been made, including a canvas by French artist Jacques Francois Lefevre (1755–1830), titled *Greek Callipyges*, and a *Metallic Venus* by Jeff Koons. Suffice to say, shapely buttocks and their sexual attractiveness have become a part of the goddess' iconography.[7]

---

7 *Deipnosophists*, XII, 554.

In 1896 the Italian criminologist Cesare Lombroso alleged that "in Greece and Rome they worshipped the spreading Venus, the *Peribasia* – the straddling or cradling, the callipygian, the oiled – to whom they offered golden phalli – and the chaste, the Venus of the sodomites." The oiled Venus may be the product of a misinterpretation: *Venus Libertina* (of freed slaves) possibly being misread for either *lubentina* (whom we met earlier in Rome) or for *lubrica* (the lubricated or slippery). The golden phalli offered to the goddess might well put us in mind of the Greek courtesan Nicias and the 'unmentionable' items she presented to a temple on her retirement. Now, whilst Lombroso was neither a classicist nor a historian, and his sources aren't clear, his collection of erotic Venuses should not seem especially unfamiliar to us by this stage: they are sexually active, dominant and diverse, although at the same time surprising us with a decidedly non-Christian approach to chasteness.[8]

Rimbaud's views of the goddess were not wholly bleak. His 1870 poem, *Sun and Flesh (Credo in Unam)*, stands in stark contrast to the grim exploitation of *Venus Anadyomene*. It is instead a hymn to Aphrodite and the fecundity of nature:

> "... when you lie down in the valley, you can smell
> How the earth is nubile and very full-blooded;
> How its huge breast, heaved up by a soul,
> Is, like God, made of love, and, like woman, of flesh,
> And that it contains, big with sap and with sunlight,
> The vast pullulation of all embryos!
> And everything grows, and everything rises!
>
> O Venus, O Goddess!
> I long for the days of antique youth,
> Of lascivious satyrs, and animal fauns,
> Gods who bit, mad with love, the bark of the boughs,

---

8 C. Lombroso, *L'Uomo Delinquente* (4th edition, 1889), vol.1, c.2, 31.

And among water-lilies kissed the nymph with fair hair!
I long for the time when the sap of the world,
River water, the rose-coloured blood of green trees
Put into the veins of Pan a whole universe!
When the earth trembled, green, beneath his goat-feet;
When, softly kissing the fair Syrinx, his lips formed
Under heaven the great hymn of love;
When, standing on the plain, he heard round about him
Living Nature answer his call."

Rimbaud also celebrates the Anatolian mother goddess Cybele, who was seen by the Romans as another form of Venus:

"Her twin breasts poured, through the vast deeps,
The pure streams of infinite life.
Mankind sucked joyfully at her blessed nipple,
Like a small child playing on her knees."

However, he mourns how, now, science and technology are making men turn from faith in the gods, giving them a proud illusion of control over the world and leading to them to abandon their faith.

"Oh! if only man still drew sustenance from your nipple,
Great mother of gods and of men, Cybele;
If only he had not forsaken immortal Astarte…"

Presciently, Rimbaud sees that humankind have disconnected themselves from their natural roots and so have fallen from grace. We hide ourselves in clothes and are ashamed of the natural beauty of our bodies and of instinctive desire and the sacredness of sex:

"And the idol in whom you placed such maidenhood,
Woman, in whom you rendered our clay divine,
So that man might bring light into his poor soul

> And slowly ascend, in unbounded love,
> From the earthly prison to the beauty of day,
> Woman no longer knows even how to be a Courtesan!
> – It's a fine farce! and the world sniggers
> At the sweet and sacred name of great Venus!"

Rimbaud hopes for salvation from the goddess, but despairs that it will come, for "Men [are] like apes, dropped from our mothers' wombs/Our feeble reason hides the infinite from us!" Still, the poet has faith that Aphrodite's love can be renewed and the old myths, of Zeus, Europa, Leda, nymphs and heroes, will come to life again and recover their power over men's hearts:

> "White Callipyge and little Eros
> Covered with the snow of rose petals, will caress
> Women and flowers beneath their lovely outstretched feet!
> … while Cypris goes by, strangely beautiful,
> And, arching the marvellous curves of her back,
> Proudly displays the golden vision of her big breasts
> And snowy belly embroidered with black moss…"

Rimbaud approaches the solution to environmental catastrophe through a vision of the Great Mother, but his general prescription for a better society is not very far from that of Æ/William Russell.

MADISON JULIUS CAWEIN

Rimbaud saw positivity in a robust sexuality, but many writers did not. Madison Cawein's vision of Aphrodite, as *The Paphian Venus*, is one that is revolted by the sexual excesses of worship on Cyprus, contrasting them starkly with a one girl's pure and steadfast love. The shrine at Paphos, the poet believes, honours:

APHRODITE – GODDESS OF MODERN LOVE

> "The Paphian goddess on her obscene throne,
> Binding all chastity to violence,
> All innocence to lust that feels no shame –
> Venus Mylitta born of filth and flame."

This goddess still seems connected to her Sumerian roots, linked to both war and lust, causing him to demand "'Can lust give birth to love? The vile and foul/ Be mother to beauty? Lo! can this thing be?" The poet presents a bleak image of Aphrodite's cult, which he rejects, although he ends on a note of hope, with a ship sighted at sea, possibly the girl's faithful lover returning.

Much of Cawein's verse was given over to dancing fairies, pretty nymphs and other appealing woodland sprites. His view of fairy tale and myth was decidedly romanticised and sweet, lacking the sense of transcendent mystery that lifted William Russell's nature spirits to a different plane. Set in this context, the aversion Cawein seems to have felt for the earthier goddess of sex should hardly surprise us. His Venus is unquestionably some bland and simpering maiden with a playful Cupid by her side – and very definitely *not* the goddess seen in Bronzino's *Allegory of Lust*, also known as *Venus and Cupid* (c.1540), in which Cupid caresses his mother's left breast, her nipple squeezed between his index and middle fingers, whilst the two kiss, her tongue darting between his lips. Deviant sexuality had no place in Cawein's cosy fantasies, but we must reconcile ourselves to the fact that Venus can be a strange mother.

A similar deity to Cawein's appears in Thomas Hardy's *The Collector Cleans His Picture*. The narrator is a rural parson, whose relief from his humdrum parish duties is his hobby collecting cheap old oil paintings and restoring them. One Saturday he sets about cleaning a new canvas he has acquired, slowly revealing a woman's features:

> "Then meseemed it the guise of the ranker Venus,
> Named of some Astarte, of some Cotytto.
> Down I knelt before it and kissed the panel,
> Drunk with the lure of love's inhibited dreamings.
>
> Till the dawn I rubbed, when there gazed up at me
> A hag, that had slowly emerged from under my hands there,
> Pointing the slanted finger towards a bosom
> Eaten away of a rot from the lusts of a lifetime –
> I could have ended myself in heart-shook horror."

This Venus is presented as a warning against lust, rather than as a symbol of pure devotion. The same is true of George Meredith's awful Venus in *To the Comic Spirit*:

> "The buxom tripper with the goblet-smile,
> Refreshful… venomous: the Dame of dames,
> Flower of the world, that honey one,
> She of the earthly rose in the sea-pearl,
> To whom the world ran ocean for her kiss…
> The lady meanwhile lures the mob, alike
> Ogles the bursters of the horn and drum.
> Curtain her close! her open arms
> Have suckers for beholders…
> Astarte of vile sweets that slay, malign,
> From Greek resplendent to Phoenician foul,
> The trader in attractions sinks, all brine
> To thoughts of taste; is 't love? Bark, dog! Hoot, owl!
> And she is blushless: ancient worship weeps.
> Suicide Graces dangle down the charms
> Sprawling like gourds on outer garden-heaps.
> She stands in her unholy oily leer
> A statue losing feature, weather-sick
> Mid draggled creepers of twined ivy sere.

> The curtain cried for magnifies to see!
> We cannot quench our one corrupting glance:
> The vision of the rumour will not flee.
> Doth the Boy own such Mother? Shoot his dart
> To bring her, countless as the crested deeps,
> Her subjects of the uncorrected heart?
> False is that vision, shrieks the devotee."

Meredith wants to divorce tainted eastern Astarte from a purer Hellenic Aphrodite, denying how much of the earlier goddess persisted in her successor. The poet sees the love brought by his Venus and Cupid as corrupted; she is a whore in an incestuous relationship with her child, alluring but untrustworthy. What Meredith doesn't seem to want to accept is her complexity, that she can accommodate loves (and lusts) of all kinds.

RICHARD LE GALLIENE

In his poem, *Alma Venus*, Le Gallienne celebrates the goddess as the bringer of Spring, thawing the ice and frosts: "She maketh ready in her hands to bring/Blossom and blade and wing." Then:

> "with her bosom all the world grow sweet,
> And blue with the sea-blue of her deep eyes
> The meadow, like another sea, shall flower,
> And all the earth be song and singing shower."

A similarly benign and maternal image is found in Le Galliene's *The House of Venus*. The goddess he praises is not "Not that Queen Venus of adulterous fame/Whose love was lust's insatiable flame," but rather "the Venus of that morning flood/With all the dawn's young passion in her blood,/With great blue eyes and unpressed bosom sweet." He prefers to conceive of her as an innocent, virgin, almost Eve-like figure.

Akin to this is Robert Laurence Binyon's *Queen Venus,* in which the goddess forsakes Olympus to sit alone on the rocky seashore, looking out over the waves. She is not, however, dreaming of the "Gardens of sultry Paphos, far away [where] Your doves among the strewn rose-petals play!" Instead, she is presented as a simple child of nature, who "comes to taste once more/ The sting and splendour of the ocean spray." It seems that sitting by the sea calms her spirit and helps her forget all the passion and pain of her life, recovering something of the innocence and freshness she felt when she was born from the ocean, "The serene charm that sets the world aflame."

ERNEST DOWSON

Dowson (1867–1900) was a consciously decadent poet, making much of his dissolute lifestyle and his preference for little girls. He liked to shock, as in his poem *Three Witches*, in which the hideous hags are called "the children of Astarte,/Dear abortions of the moon," a memorably Gothic invocation of the Phoenician goddess. However, in *Libera Me* he implores the goddess to help him after a life of indulgence and excess, all enjoyed in her name. His is a burned-out shell, worn out by passion:

"Goddess the laughter-loving, Aphrodite, befriend!
Long have I served thine altars, serve me now at the end,
Let me have peace of thee, truce of thee, golden one, send.

Heart of my heart have I offered thee, pain of my pain,
Yielding my life for the love of thee into thy chain;
Lady and goddess be merciful, loose me again.

All things I had that were fairest, my dearest and best,
Fed the fierce flames on thine altar: ah, surely, my breast
Shrined thee alone among goddesses, spurning the rest.

Blossom of youth thou hast plucked of me, flower of my
    days;
Stinted I nought in thine honouring, walked in thy ways,
Song of my soul pouring out to thee, all in thy praise.

Fierce was the flame while it lasted, and strong was thy wine,
Meet for immortals that die not, for throats such as thine,
Too fierce for bodies of mortals, too potent for mine.

Blossom and bloom hast thou taken, now render to me
Ashes of life that remain to me, few though they be,
Truce of the love of thee, Cyprian, let me go free.

Goddess the laughter-loving, Aphrodite, restore
Life to the limbs of me, liberty, hold me no more
Having the first-fruits and flower of me, cast me the core.

The lifestyle chosen by Dowson in his youth was also envisaged by George Meredith in his poem *The Vital Choice*. Humans have two options, a chaste familial life or hedonistic pleasure – although both lead to the same conclusion:

"Or shall we run with Artemis
Or yield the breast to Aphrodite?
Both are mighty;
Both give bliss;
Each can torture if divided;
Each claims worship undivided,
In her wake would have us wallow.

Youth must offer on bent knees
Homage unto one or other;
Earth, the mother,
This decrees;
And unto the pallid scyther
Either points us, shun we either,
Shun or too devoutly follow."

ALGERNON SWINBURNE

Aphrodite has always brought pain just as much as she has been responsible for joy. The Sicilian Greek poet Ibykos, writing in the sixth century BCE, described love as a dark north wind flashing with lightning. The goddess sent it to bring madness and despair to hapless victims.

Algernon Charles Swinburne (1837–1909), just like both Ibykos and Ernest Dowson, seemed to understand the bitter costs of love and of devotion to a cruel lover. Several of Swinburne's poems view love as the cause of all human pain. In his imitation of the 'sapphic metre,' the *Sapphics* of 1866, the goddess is "white implacable Aphrodite" (albeit one shaken with weeping as she leaves Sappho on Lesbos). The poet's *Atalanta in Calydon*, published in the previous year, sets out the indictment against the deity very clearly. He begins in benign terms:

> "She is fair, she is white like a dove,
> And the life of the world in her breath
> Breathes, and is born at her birth;
> For they knew thee for mother of love…"

For the poet, though, Aphrodite is "mother of death," a "perilous goddess" and "mother of strife." This is because of her 'dart and sting and thorn;' love is a curse, the source of all woes and suffering. He asks why it is:

"That thou, having wings as a dove,
Being girt with desire for a girth,
That thou must come after these,
That thou must lay on him love?"[9]

Swinburne's poem *Dolores* is addressed to just such a heartless woman, whom he elevates to semi-divine status as 'Our Lady of Pain (or of Torture).' The verse is a lament and accusation for "the loves that complete and control/All the joys of the flesh, all the sorrows/That wear out the soul." His uncaring idol has ensnared him with "the raptures and roses of vice" and he has offered "the cypress to love… the myrtle to death."

Part of what made Swinburne so popular and controversial in his time was his daring sexual imagery, hinting at perverse and unhealthy passions. It was deliciously suggestive, whilst being learned and deeply poetic. *Dolores*, for example, is replete with allusive imagery indicative of Aphrodite, albeit a version of the deity whose "love is more cruel than lust," with whom "virtues are vices." References to her roses abound, but she is scarcely addressed directly. Swinburne calls his tormenter Thalassian (born of the waves). She has risen "foam white" from the sea, but this apparent purity is illusory:

"The white wealth of thy body made whiter
By the blushes of amorous blows,
And seamed with sharp lips and fierce fingers,
And branded by kisses that bruise."

Dolores, the harsh mistress and dominant lover, is "lithe and lascivious," her "hair loosened and soiled in mid orgies/With kisses and wine." However, these condemnations change and resolve themselves towards the end of the poem, where Swinburne begins to lament the displacement of the pagan gods

---
[9] Swinburne, *Atalanta in Calydon*, Chorus: 'We have seen thee, O Love.'

by Christianity, the replacement of Venus by Mary – a "goddess new-born" – and the defamation of the Olympians' names. So it is that the poet asks:

> "Where are they, Cotytto or Venus,
> Astarte or Ashtaroth, where?
> Do their hands as we touch come between us?
> Is the breath of them hot in thy hair?
> From their lips have thy lips taken fever,
> With the blood of their bodies grown red?
> Hast thou left upon earth a believer
> If these men are dead?
>
> They were purple of raiment and golden,
> Filled full of thee, fiery with wine,
> Thy lovers, in haunts unbeholden,
> In marvellous chambers of thine.
> They are fled, and their footprints escape us,
> Who appraise thee, adore, and abstain,
> O daughter of Death and Priapus,
> Our Lady of Pain.
>
> What ails us to fear overmeasure,
> To praise thee with timorous breath,
> O mistress and mother of pleasure,
> The one thing as certain as death?"

Swinburne therefore concluded redemptively, suggesting that pagan celebration may be as valid a way of living as being virtuous – but full of guilt over bodily pleasure. He pursued this same theme in *Hymn to Proserpine*, which is spoken by a pagan priest in Rome, berating the official endorsement of the Christian faith by the imperial authorities. The narrator only has contempt for the joylessness of the new religion, which lacks:

> "The laurel, palms and the paean, the breasts of the nymphs in the brake;
> Breasts more soft than a dove's, that tremble with tenderer breath;
> And all the wings of the Loves, and all the joy before death."

Because it values life after death more highly than life on earth, the new church has nothing to offer that equals these pleasures, the speaker claims. As a result, it shall pass away too in time: it cannot compete with the power and beauty of Aphrodite:

> "Though before thee the throned Cytherean be fallen, and hidden her head,
> Yet thy kingdom shall pass, Galilean, thy dead shall go down to thee dead.
> Of the maiden thy mother men sing as a goddess with grace clad around;
> Thou art throned where another was king; where another was queen she is crowned.
> Yea, once we had sight of another: but now she is queen, say these.
> Not as thine, not as thine was our mother, a blossom of flowering seas,
> Clothed round with the world's desire as with raiment, and fair as the foam,
> And fleeter than kindled fire, and a goddess, and mother of Rome.
> For thine came pale and a maiden, and sister to sorrow; but ours,
> Her deep hair heavily laden with odour and colour of flowers,
> White rose of the rose-white water, a silver splendour, a flame,

> Bent down unto us that besought her, and earth grew sweet with her name.
> For thine came weeping, a slave among slaves, and rejected; but she
> Came flushed from the full-flushed wave, and imperial, her foot on the sea.
> And the wonderful waters knew her, the winds and the viewless ways,
> And the roses grew rosier, and bluer the sea-blue stream of the bays."

Aphrodite is more appealing because she is a mother to all and sponsor of love. This age-old tension between the church and the physical passions of Venus is found too in Swinburne's 1866 poem, *Laus Veneris*. The title means 'The Praise of Venus' and is based on the theme of Richard Wagner's opera *Tannhäuser*, which is in turn derives from the myth of Venus and her palace under the Venusberg mountain. In the legend, the young knight Tannhäuser falls in love with Venus and lives with her in her faery realm until he becomes so overwhelmed by remorse at his fleshly sins that he makes a pilgrimage to Rome to seek absolution. This is denied to him as being impossible. The entire tone of the poem is one of hopeless regret: the love and sex with Venus was all consuming at the time, but it later turns bitter. Nonetheless, the knight struggles between the attraction of her physical joys and the redemption offered by the church.

The goddess of Swinburne's *Laus Veneris* is "the world's delight" and her bodily charms are an almost irresistible but terrible temptation, with which the church can scarcely contend:

> "Alas, Lord, surely thou art great and fair.
> But lo her wonderfully woven hair!
> And thou didst heal us with thy piteous kiss;
> But see now, Lord; her mouth is lovelier…

> Had now thy mother such a lip – like this?
> Thou knowest how sweet a thing it is to me."

Passion with Venus is intense but ultimately, perhaps, unsatisfying:

> "Brief bitter bliss, one hath for a great sin;
> Nathless thou knowest how sweet a thing it is."

The young knight sees Venus first under a (fairy) elder tree, "Naked, with hair shed over to the knee" (this erotic obsession with thick hair is something the poet shared with Rossetti and which the latter portrayed repeatedly in his female figures). This faery queen is beautiful beyond compare and cannot be denied:

> "As when she came out of the naked sea
> Making the foam as fire whereon she trod,
> And as the inner flower of fire was she.
>
> Yea, she laid hold upon me, and her mouth
> Clove unto mine as soul to body doth,
> And, laughing, made her lips luxurious;
> Her hair had smells of all the sunburnt south,
>
> Strange spice and flower, strange savour of crushed fruit
> And perfume…
> And I forgot fear and all weary things…
> Feeling her face with all her eager hair
> Cleave to me, clinging as a fire that clings…
>
> Ah love, there is no better life than this;
> To have known love, how bitter a thing it is…"

Swinburne struggled throughout his life with his physical desires (he was a masochist) and with the ingrained sense of sin and self-denial that the church had instilled in him. Venus represents a means of liberating self-expression – and self-acceptance.

One last poem by Swinburne should be mentioned, although it is a slight detour from our main theme. This is *Hermaphroditus*, written in March 1863 after viewing the ancient Greek statue of the sleeping hermaphrodite on display in the Louvre in Paris. The figure is that of a naked young woman, reclining on her side. She presents to the viewer a shapely bottom and, from the front, breasts and male genitals. Swinburne was inspired to examine the figure's state of mind, after "thy limbs melted into Salmacis… And all thy boy's breath softened into sighs." The verse is sensuous, but ambiguous; the poet seems baffled by what he sees – "To what strange end hath some strange god made fair/The double blossom of two fruitless flowers?" The sight is erotic:

> "Two loves at either blossom of thy breast
> Strive until one be under and one above.
> Thy breath is fire upon the amorous air,
> Fire in thy eyes and where thy lips suspire…
>
> Sex to sweet sex with limbs and lips is wed…"

But the result is (quite literally) fruitless, generating only the "waste wedlock of a sterile kiss." The figure inspires both great desire *and* great despair.

Aphrodite's double child is a puzzling and frustrating image and writers and artists have been fascinated throughout history. At the conclusion of a poetry reading in Massachusetts in early 1950, Dylan Thomas asked his audience – "If a hermaphrodite were a schizophrene, which half would you take?" Throughout his life Thomas played with mentions of hermaphrodites in his poetry, prose, correspondence and conversation. In one of his very earliest poems, from 1931, he described a lover as his "hermaphrodite in logic" with whom loves turns in a ring, "from tip to cavity," so that, in their "cerebral sodomy," he will "force

[her] to a different sex." The possibilities and imagery intrigued the poet intellectually, although – Thomas being Thomas – at one academic dinner in the US he was asked why he had expressed a desire to be hermaphrodite and replied "so we can all f**k ourselves."

MARINA TSVETAEVA

The Russian poet, Tsvetaeva (1892–1941), wrote her *Praise to Aphrodite* in October 1921. The poem describes her conscious efforts to escape the 'feminine' and romantic aspects associated with the goddess, choosing instead combat and sport, which seemed more worthy to her than love and passively "giving bliss." Aphrodite and her ways were something that she had outgrown – with her youth – and so she rejected the flocks of cooing doves, "the voluptuous belt" and "the beloved myrtle."

> "Shooting hard with a blunt arrow,
> Your own son rescued me.
> Thus, around the throne of my languor
> What was born of foam will vanish in foam!
>
> … Every cloud in evil times
> Is curved like a breast.
> Your face is in every innocent flower,
> She-Devil!
>
> Perishable foam, sea salt…
> In reproach and in torment –
> For how long do we obey you,
> Armless stone?"

The goddess of love was a distraction for a rational, revolutionary society. The modern world no longer needed her – a utilitarian sentiment expressed later by British poet Dannie Abse in his verse *The Old Gods*:

> "The gods, old as night, don't trouble us.
> Poor weeping Venus! Her pubic hairs are grey,
> and her magic love girdle has lost its spring…
>
> All the old gods have become enfeebled,
> mere playthings for poets…"

Perhaps, after the millennium, our experience of preceding century may mean that we are less prepared to reject myth and to embrace cold reason.

CLARK ASHTON SMITH

Smith (1893–1961) is best known as a writer of horror fiction, in the mould of H. P. Lovecraft. However, he was a poet, too, and an autodidact with a fascination for classical myths, something of which can be seen reflected in his elaborate diction. His verse is scattered with references to Aphrodite, as in *Eidolon*, in which the idolised (but possibly illusory) woman of the title is praised as "More beautiful than any sphinx, and fair/As Aphrodite dead." The goddess appears in *Masque of Forsaken Gods* in classic form, combining the joys and the tortures of love:

> "I, born of sound and foam,
> Child of the sea and wind,
> Was fire upon mankind –
> Fuelled with Syria, and with Greece and Rome.
> Time fanned me with his breath,
> Love found new warmth in me,
> And Life its ecstasy,
> Till I grew deadly with the wind of death."

Smith was also keenly aware of the role of the son of the goddess, Eros-Cupid, and of the other *Erotes*, and addressed several poems to them as "Lord[s] of the many pangs, the single ecstasy!"[10]

Even so, for Smith, Venus-Aphrodite is, first and foremost, the goddess of life-affirming love and the divinity who will answer the prayers of lovers:[11]

"Grant O Venus

Though love had dreamt of soft eternities
For never-flagging pulses still to mete,
Those minutes of our bliss were few and fleet.
Breast-pillowed in their aftermath of ease,
She said to me at midnight: 'Memories
Are all we have in the end.' Ah, bitter-sweet
The doom that tolling bells of thought repeat –
This verity of solemn verities
Wherein the sorrowful senses find despair
And the heart an iridescence on dark tears…

But grant, O Venus of the hidden hill,
That many a rose-lit eve remain to share,
And midnights in the unascended years,
And starry memories unbegotten still."

The poet seems – like others – to question the cultural expectation of a single enduring love in each person's life, but he does acknowledge the existence of spells of joy with lovers, not least those of post-coital closeness. As for his 'Venus of the hidden hill,' I'm not sure here if we're discussing Tannhäuser's faery realm beneath the Venusberg, or Aphrodite as goddess of physical love and the *mons veneris*.

---

10 See *Eros of Ebony; Farewell to Eros; The Crucifixion of Eros.*
11 See too *To George Sterling: A Valediction* and *The Hill of Dionysus.*

Smith also wrote plays, short stories and 'prose poems.' From his fragmentary drama *Aphrodite and the Priest*, we have this description of the goddess as she tries to tempt the holy man. She appears to him in extravagantly sexy form, as:

> "a woman fair and voluptuous as the first dreams of puberty, and naked as an antique statue. Her breasts and arms are moulded in the solemn, superb, inevitable lines of a divine lasciviousness; and her hair is like morning on a waterfall; her eyes are the sapphires bathed in wine. She smiles, and in the curve of her crescent lips ineffable lore is manifest, as if an entire *kalpa* of summers were epitomised in a single rose. With open arms, she advances…"

This is all the power and allure of the goddess manifest and unvanquishable. However, in his short prose-poem *The Passing of Aphrodite*, Smith imagined the goddess leaving her classical homelands, her departure across the sea named Oblivion being witnessed by a poet called Phaniol. A boat bearing two noble women appears and he enquires why they are there:

> 'We wait the goddess Aphrodite, who departs in weariness and sorrow… from all the lands of this world of petty loves and pettier mortalities. Thou, because thou art a poet, and hast known the great sovereignty of love, shall behold her departure. But they, the men of the court, the marketplace and the temple, shall receive no message nor sign of her going-forth, and will scarcely dream that she is gone… Now, O Phaniol, the time, the goddess and the going-forth are at hand.'
>
> Even as they ceased, One came across the desert; and her coming was a light on the far hills; and where she trod the lengthening shadows shrunk, and the grey waste put on the purple asphodels and the deep verdure it had worn when those queens were young, that now are a darkening

> legend and a dust of mummia. Even to the shore she came and stood before Phaniol, while the sunset greatened, filling sky and sea with a flush as of new-blown blossoms, or the inmost rose of that coiling shell which was consecrate to her in old time. Without robe or circlet or garland, crowned and clad only with the sunset, fair with the dreams of man but fairer yet than all dreams...
>
> 'Farewell, O Phaniol,' she said... 'I go, and when I am gone, thou shalt worship still and shalt not know me. For the destinies are thus, and not forever to any man, to any world or to any god, is it given to possess me wholly. Autumn and spring will return when I am past, the one with yellow leaves, the other with yellow violets; birds will haunt the renewing myrtles; and many little loves will be thine. Not again to thee or to any man will return the perfect vision and the perfect flesh of the goddess."

With her departure, the flowers fade, darkness falls and Phaniol is left bereft.

Clark Ashton Smith taught himself French so that he could read – and then translate – the poetry of the leading Symbolist writer Charles Baudelaire. Smith's own verse, *On Re-Reading Baudelaire,* conjures the mental images invoked by reading the great poet's work: it is a catalogue of flowers from classical myth – lilies, lotus, laurel, ivy, rose, hellebore, amaranth and "wan myrtles with acrid, sick perfume... some fleeting fragrance [which] lures us in the gloom/To Paphian dells or vales of Proserpine..."

As for Baudelaire himself, his *Voyage To Cythera* is Gothically dark description of a pilgrimage to one of the great shrines of the goddess:

> "... 'That dark, grim island there – which would that be?'
> 'Cythera,' we're told, 'the legendary isle

Old bachelors tell stories of and smile.
There's really not much to it, you can see.'

O place of many a mystic sacrament!
Archaic Aphrodite's splendid shade
Lingers above your waters like a scent
Infusing spirits with an amorous mood.

Worshipped from of old by every nation,
Myrtle-green isle, where each new bud discloses
Sighs of souls in loving adoration
Breathing like incense from a bank of roses

Or like a dove coo-cooing endlessly…
No; Cythera was a poor infertile rock,
A stony desert harrowed by the shriek
Of gulls. And yet there was something to see:

This was no temple deep in flowers and trees
With a young priestess moving to and fro,
Her body heated by a secret glow,
Her robe half-opening to every breeze;

But coasting nearer, close enough to land
To scatter flocks of birds as we passed by,
We saw a tall cypress-shaped thing at hand –
A triple gibbet black against the sky."

The grisly sight of a hanged corpse, ravaged by seagulls, instead of a sexy priestess, jolts the poet into reflecting upon his own mortality:

"O Venus! On your isle what did I see
But my own image on the gallows tree?
O God, give me the strength to contemplate
My own heart, my own body without hate!"

STEVIE SMITH

British poet and novelist, Stevie Smith (1902–71), discussing her unsatisfactory love life, said of herself, "I have never neglected the altars of Venus nor avoided her *supplices*, certainly I rate this goddess very highly and have never refused an encounter, nor treated her so impiously as [some]…"

Sadly, though, she never found a long-standing love in her own life. Worse still, perhaps, Smith felt that the goddess was a severe mistress, judging her harshly for continually choosing the wrong men: "Venus was very *farouche* [fierce] and furious. Very *farouche* and furious indeed was Venus: 'Well Miss, you've brought it upon yourself and now you'll please to suffer for it.'"[12]

Smith was well-read, in both the classics and European literature, a learning she displayed lightly in a poem such as *Phèdre* in which she imagined a comic alternative and happy ending to the myth of Phaedra and Hippolytus. This was one in which the couple were able to marry –

> "and everything would have been respectable
> and the wretched Venus could have lumped it,
> Lumped, I mean, Phèdre
> Being the only respectable member
> Of her awful family
> And being happy."

Smith remarked, in *Novel on Yellow Paper*, that the Greeks "made a temple to the backside of Venus; that, anyone who knows what a fine thing sex is, knows." She also cited Lucretius' *Invocation to Venus*, "Quæ quoniam rerum naturam sola gubernas…" as one of her favourite quotations. In full, the Latin author had addressed the goddess thus:

---

12 Smith, *Novel on Yellow Paper*, 1936 (Penguin 1972) 129 & 144.

> "*Since you alone rule over the nature of things,* since without you nothing emerges into the immense radiance of the world, indeed nothing joyous nor beautiful is born, I honour you in crafting these verses... Goddess, I beseech you to grant my words an ever-lasting appeal. Moreover, let this come to pass: on all the seas and lands of our earth, may the savage works of war be stilled, and let there be peace."[13]

Perhaps surprisingly for a single woman of her time, Stevie Smith openly spoke about – and praised – Venus as the goddess of sexual pleasure.

Mostly, though, Smith's view of Venus linked her with death, an aspect that was familiar to the Greeks. She was known variously as Aphrodite *Epitymbia* (of the tombs), *Tymborychos* (grave digger), *Muchia* (of the depths) and *Melainis* (the dark one). These associations seem to relate to her role as a goddess of renewal and regrowth in Spring and to her lover Adonis, who spent part of the year in the underworld, before being born again. Aphrodite's ancestor, Ishtar, also had a partner, called Dumuzi (or Tammuz), who spent half the year in the land of the dead.

So, in Smith's poem *Votaries of Both Sexes Cry First to Venus*, death is equated with love and its calm and peace are contrasted to the torments of "Crying for pleasure/Crying for pain/Longing to see you again and again":

> "But one stood up and said: I love
> The love that comes in the dark fields.
> In the late night, in the hot breathless dark night:
> In the moony forest, when there is a moon,
> In the moony rides of the dark forest.

---

13 *Novel on Yellow Paper*, 22 & 28; Titus Lucretius Caro, *De rerum natura*, Book 1, 21–30.

I love this love: it is eerie if there is not
My love in my arms then. It is exciting then,
It is such an excitement as is on the approach
Of Death..."

The same imagery is found in Smith's poem, *Venus When Young Choosing Death*, in which the goddess prefers the enfolding consolations of death (or sleep) over the adoration of friends and supplicants. Readers might note, as well, that intoxication with opium seems to have been an aspect of Greek ceremonies in praise of Aphrodite:

"I stood knee deep in the sea
I saw gods coming towards me
All came and kissed, all kissed
It was for friendship...

Then came out drawing a boat after him
He set me in the boat
He set me on his knees in the boat, kissing me.
It was not for friendship.

Oh, how happy this day was
All day in his arms I was,
But not for friendship.

A little breeze drew now from the land
Bringing a smell of poppies
And on his head, was poppies
And in his hand, poppies
And on his lips when he kissed me
A taste of poppies.

Sleep or Death, Sleep or Death kissed me,
Not for friendship.

You do not kiss one for friendship?
No, for welcome,
To welcome one home."

In contrast, C.S. Lewis was aware of the same links to mortality, but in his view the goddess was a means of overcoming death. His poem, *Le Roi S'Amuse* depicts Jove/Zeus creating the world and the different Olympian gods; for Lewis, Aphrodite represented the positive aspects of the human spirit – joy, hope and confidence in the future:

"The hoving tide of
Ocean trembled at the motion of his breath.
The sigh turned
Into white, eternal,
Radiant Aphrodite unafraid of death;
A fragrance, a vagrant unrest on earth she flung,
There was favouring and fondling and bravery and building
and chuckling music and suckling of the young."

W.H. AUDEN

Auden (1907–73) was perceptive as to the vital role in human affairs of the love goddess and her attendants. She is the motive force driving creativity, but she is also disruptive and disturbing. He concludes his verse *In Memory of Sigmund Freud* with these lines:

"Over his grave
the household of Impulse mourns one dearly loved:
sad is Eros, builder of cities,
and weeping anarchic Aphrodite."

These lines incorporate elements of Freud's psycho-analytic theories, but they also acknowledge the deeper cultural role of the goddess. A similar perception of her function lies behind Auden's *Venus Will Now Say a Few Words* of 1929, although here she seems to be cast more as creator of the universe, displacing the Judeo-Christian god:

> "Since you are going to begin today
> Let us consider what it is you do…
> Relax in your darling's arms like a stone…
> Making the most of firelight, of hours and fuss;
> But joy is mine not yours – to have come so far,
> Whose cleverest invention was lately fur…
> To reach that shape for your face to assume,
> Pleasure to many and despair to some,
> I shifted ranges…
> Altered desire and history of dress."[14]

Venus goes on to remind her listeners that everything will pass away – them, their lovers and, even, their civilisation. She is still the patron of lovers though, as we see in *Lullaby*:

> "To lovers as they lie upon
> Her tolerant enchanted slope
> In their ordinary swoon,
> Grave the vision Venus sends
> Of supernatural sympathy,
> Universal love and hope."

Even so, there is a sense of transience and impermanence here: Venus is 'grave' in that her message is serious, but she may be reminding the lovers of their mortality too, just as did Stevie Smith's goddess.

---

14 May the reference here to fur allude not just to her power as creator of animals but also to *Venus in Furs* (for which see next chapter)?

In his lyric for Benjamin Britten's *Hymn to St Cecilia*, the 1942 adaptation of his anthem to the saint, Auden mingles pagan and Christian elements, as well as introducing music into her mythology:

> "Blonde Aphrodite rose up excited,
> Moved to delight by the melody,
> White as an orchid she rode quite naked
> In an oyster shell on top of the sea
> At sounds so entrancing the angels dancing
> Came out of their trance into time again."

It may seem odd to find the nude goddess in a choral piece for churches, but we have already seen how the myths of Venus accommodated themselves with the new faith. It is another tribute to her enduring and irrepressible power.

SYLVIA PLATH

American poet Sylvia Plath (1932–63) addressed another aspect of the love goddess that tends to receive less attention in the arts. In her 1961 poem, *Heavy Women*, she casts a cynical gaze at pregnant women, unimpressed (it seems) by their aura of maternal self-satisfaction:

> "Irrefutable, beautifully smug
> As Venus, pedestalled on a half-shell
> Shawled in blond hair and the salt
> Scrim of a sea breeze, the women
> Settle in their belling dresses.
> Over each weighty stomach a face
> Floats calm as a moon or a cloud."

These gravid women smile to themselves, as "pink-buttocked infants" play nearby, a clear echo of the gambolling cupids that often surround Venus in pictures. The women seem aimless, awaiting the birth of their children, but they "step among the archetypes, [as] Dusk hoods them in Mary-blue." Plath reminds us here that Venus and the Virgin Mary have their historical connections.

Kathleen Raine (1908–2003) also recognised that women bore, in themselves, aspects of Aphrodite and of many other archetypal goddesses. Each woman, during her life, can be mother, lover and, ultimately mortal, and she will know successively pain, joy and grief:

> "Strange that the self's continuum should outlast
> The Virgin, Aphrodite, and the Mourning Mother,
> All loves and griefs, successive deities
> That hold their kingdom in the human breast...
> And I who have been Virgin and Aphrodite,
> The mourning Isis and the queen of corn
> Wait for the last mummer, dread Persephone
> To dance my dust at last into the tomb."[15]

Just like the goddess, each woman herself is part of a natural cycle of renewal and decay. Life will grow, die and reappear – as indeed may love.

GEOFFREY GRIGSON

Grigson (1905–85) has been mentioned already in this book as author of a study of Aphrodite, *The Goddess of Love*. He documented his fascination with the deity in his poetry, too, recording a visit to her bathing place on Cyprus (*The Cyprian's*

---

15 Raine, *Transit of the Gods*.

Spring) or remarking how her two eyes are painted for protection on the prows of Greek fishing boats (*The Oculi*).

His most poignant piece, though, is his 1976 verse, *Bright Piece Out of the Sea*. A statue of Aphrodite is recovered from the beneath the waves and hauled unceremoniously ashore after 1700 years:

> "... Saints – that was our fathers'
> Name for them – clapped when Greeks stole
> Gold laces from her neck, then, I admit
> Not dragging her sweet backside over her
> Stony temenos or bruising her sweet fixed
> Smile, carried her to the edge with care
> And pitched her from this highest headland...
>
> Give her a black pedestal in the best
> Museum room. Publish a postcard. Establish
> White doves in a cote outside. A television
> Eye will see you if you begin to pencil
> Your name with your girl's name across her
> Formerly pink thigh. But observe: most
> Days this dead museum is shut. Her white
> Doves have become grey. The Graces do
> Not attend. She cannot dance with them
> And now she has not a thing to say."

The goddess has been recovered from the oblivion she was cast into by puritans, but displaying her as an art object and preventing people interacting with her, leaves Aphrodite lifeless and cut-off. Her power comes when people can make contact with her – as well as with each other.

CONCLUSION

Venus and the other female goddesses of love, sex and fecundity are ingrained symbolically, deep within the narratives of our culture. Even the most allusive mentions of them can be sufficient to trigger powerful associations and emotions. British poet, David Jones, in poem *Sherethursday and Venus day,* achieves this with only the briefest of mentions: "He that was her son/is now her lover;" "poor Ishtar is a-weeping in the burning sun of day." Jones densely interweaves references to the cult of the Great Mother, to Dionysus, and to the liberated sexuality of the classical myths – "loosener of the naiad girdles" – to produce an intense new mythology of his own. He shows how these ancient characters and stories can still have urgent meaning.[16]

Aphrodite, as the goddess of romantic love and of the pangs associated with devotion, has been an abiding subject for poetry. Nonetheless, the last one hundred and fifty years or so have seen new themes being emphasised. More modern audiences are interested in Aphrodite as universal mother, as sexually liberated woman, as a symbol of sexual diversity and as a figure suggestive of erotic power and domination. It is in this more complex and robust form that the twenty first century has inherited her.

---

16 David Jones, *The Anathemata,* 1952.

The Goddess in Prose

In this section I shall focus on two novelists primarily: Pierre Louys and Leopold von Sacher-Masoch, whose late nineteenth century work has had the most profound impact on our perceptions of Venus-Aphrodite over the succeeding century. Often the name of the goddess has been used by authors merely for allusion, as in Laurence Durrell's *Revolt of Aphrodite* (1968–70). A female character in his story dies and is resurrected as a robot, a clear reference to Galatea, the statute carved by Pygmalion and brought to life by Aphrodite.

Sally Vickers' *Aphrodite's Hat* (2011) is an acclaimed collection of love stories. The story that gives the volume its title concerns two married people conducting an affair. They meet at lunch times in London's National Gallery, where we first encounter them, standing before Lucas Cranach the Elder's *Cupid Complaining to Venus*. The goddess in the picture is "undeniably erotic" with her elegant pose and small breasts. Her nakedness is offset by some heavy necklaces and by a large and elaborate fur-trimmed hat. Vickers suggests that Venus' message is that nudity is good, but that you shouldn't be too exposed.[1]

In addition to these literary works, there is also an enormous amount of romantic and erotic fiction using the name of the goddess. Self-publishing on the internet seems to have multiplied the supply of these enormously, as any glance at the Amazon website will suggest, but the trend is far from new. A book titled *Venus in India* was published in 1869 by a 'Charles Devereaux.' It presents itself as an account of the experiences

---

1 Cranach painted numerous pictures of Venus – the National Gallery also holds a slightly later *Venus and Cupid*; others may be found in Geneva and Frankfurt. In Karlsruhe, there is also Cranach's *Judgment of Paris*; in all of these, the hat features prominently, emphasising her bare state.

of a British Army doctor serving on the North West Frontier of India. He has left his wife behind in England, telling the reader that "I made no promise of fidelity [because] the idea seemed never to occur... of there being any need for it, for although I had always been of that temperament so dear to Venus, and had enjoyed the pleasure of love with great good fortune before I married, yet I had, as I thought, quite steadied down into a proper married man, whose desires never wandered outside his own bed." However, within a few lines Devereaux has to confess that "Little did I think [that] there were waiting for me, in glowing India, all unknown and unsuspected, other voluptuous women, whose beautiful naked charms were to form my couch, and whose lovely limbs were to bind me in ecstatic embrace... Thanks be to tender Venus for having raised an imperious cloud, and hidden my sportings with my nymphs..." Soon enough, then, he finds himself a young lover whose "freshness, beauty, and all that excites desire, could not have existed in any body but that of the great Mother of love, Venus herself." She is, indeed, a "perfect priestess of Venus." In fact, a succession of erotic encounters follow with the daughters of British servants of the Raj, all praised for their goddess-like charms.

JOHN DONNE

As we saw at the close of the first chapter of this book, Venus-Aphrodite entered the Christian era with a poor reputation with the church. She may have been divine, but she was a loose woman and contemptible for that. Such an attitude took a long time to dissipate, as may be seen from a work by John Donne (1572–1631). Although some of his youthful verse was subtly erotic, Donne was appointed Dean of St Paul's Cathedral in London and, over time, became increasingly pious.

Donne's *Paradoxes, problemes, essayes, characters*, published posthumously in 1652, comprises a series of queries and conundrums. One of his questions is *"Why Venus-star only doth cast a shadow?"* His explanation is to wonder whether it is because "the works of Venus want shadowing, covering, and disguising." He continues:

> "Venus' markets [ways] are so natural, that when we solicite the best way (which is by marriage) our perswasions work not so much to draw a woman to us, as against her nature to draw her from all other besides. And so, when we go against nature, and from Venus' work (for marriage is chastitie) we need shadowes and colours, but not else. In Seneca's time it was a course, an un-Roman and a contemptible thing even in a Matron, not to have had a Love beside her husband, which though the Law required not at their hands, yet they did it zealously out of the Councel of Custom and fashion, which was venery of supererogation [over and above the call of duty]: 'the adulterer delights you more than a spectator,' saith Martial."

Donne approached Venus with a jaundiced eye: she is the natural enemy of good morals by provoking lusts and curiosity. He had attacked her as the enemy of constancy and monogamy as early as the 1590s in his poem *The Indifferent*. In fact, her influence was even worse than that, as the answer to his next question disclosed:

> "Venus is multinominous [many-named] to give example to her prostitute disciples, who so often, either to renew or refresh themselves towards lovers, or to disguise themselves from Magistrates, are to take new names. It may be she takes new names after her many functions, for as she is supream Monarch of all Suns at large (which is lust) so is she joyned in Commission with all Mythologicks, with Iuno, Diana, and all others for marriage. It may be because of the

divers names to herself, for her affections have more names than any vice: *scilicet*, Pollution, Fornication, Adultery, Lay-Incest, Church-Incest, Rape, Sodomy, Mastupration, Masturbation, and a thousand others. Perchance her divers names shewed her appliableness to divers men, for Neptune distilled and wet her in love, the Sun warms and melts her, Mercury perswaded and swore her, Jupiter's authority secured, and Vulcan hammer'd her. As Hesperus she presents you with her *bonum utile* [useful qualities], because it is wholesomest in the morning: As Vesper with her *bonum delectabile* [delightful qualities], because it is pleasantest in the evening. And because industrious men rise and endure with the Sun in their civil businesses, this Star calls them up a little before, and remembers them again a little after for her business; for certainly, '*Venit Hesperus, ite capelle*' [Evening comes, go to chapel]: was spoken to Lovers in the persons of Goats."

Donne's English and Latin may be a little hard to follow nowadays, but the gist is clear: Venus is a corrupting influence in his opinion. She leads humans into fornication in all its varied and delightful forms – in which context we might note Ben Jonson's saucy joke, in his poem *Venus' Runaway*, that whoever finds the errant Cupid "Shall to-night receive a kiss/How or where herself would wish." Donne regards the adherents of the goddess as no more than prostitutes; all that anyone under her influence thinks about is sex. Lastly, though he is a senior cleric, I feel sure that Donne's mention of Venus made wet by Neptune, and then hammered by Vulcan, should be assumed to bear the subtext we still read into it today.[2]

---

2 *Paradoxes, problemes, essayes, characters written by Dr. Donne, Dean of Pauls*, Problems, 8 & 9.

PIERRE LOUYS

Pierre Louys (1870–1925) was a French poet and writer. He was born Pierre Louis in Ghent, but his family soon moved to Paris, where he remained for the rest of his life. Calling himself Louÿs, he wrote his first erotic texts aged eighteen, when he was much influenced by the Symbolists.

In 1891, Louÿs helped found a literary review, *La Conque*, in which he published *Astarte*, a collection of his early erotic verse. This he followed up in 1894 with a further erotic collection – the one hundred and forty-three prose poems called *Les Chansons de Bilitis*. This was followed in 1896 by his first novel, *Aphrodite – mœurs antiques*, which proved a best seller. Louÿs went on to publish *Les Aventures du roi Pausole* in 1901 and continued to compose obscene erotic texts until his death.

A reconstructed classical world and sexual (especially lesbian) attraction are themes which ran throughout his life's work, as the following verse, *Eros*, demonstrates. In it we see the goddess and son, alongside an orgy of other mythological beings:

> "Deep in the lurking shadows of the woods,
> Down vistas gold-flecked from the sunlight glare
> The satyrs fast pursue the oreads.
> Clutching their virgin breasts and flying hair,
> Bending their gleaming bodies, tense with fear,
> Swift backward on the damp moss. Half divine,
> Writhing with pain…
> O Women! On your soft lips, Eros cries
> 'Desires and agonies.'
> 'Eros! Eros!'
>
> Cybele long pursues across the plains
> The godlike Attis whom her love desires,
> The fleeting Attis who her love disdains

For Eros, like a cruel god, conspires
To chill return where burning love aspires,
And, in despair, through Attis' halting breath,
Cybele weaves of death…
Slaying with tortured cries,
Desires and agonies…
'Eros! Eros!'

Before the goat-foot, over the flowery meads –
Toward the water tomb, frail Syrinx speeds,
Shuddering at Eros' kiss upon her cheek –
Eros who, later, culls the trembling reeds,
Caresses them and, living, makes them speak
For he who conquers Gods, who death disdains –
Pale Eros-reigns…
O women! From a dead soul, Eros cries
'Desires and agonies.'

In this verse, Louys makes free with tradition, for the Great Mother, Cybele, who is accompanied by her youthful lover Attis, is mixed in with satyrs, nymphs, Pan and, of course, Eros, son of Aphrodite. Just as he invented his own mythology, Louys created his own version of history, as we shall see in his two most famous works.

Aphrodite

Sexuality and religious prostitution are at the core of Pierre Louys first novel, *Aphrodite*, which was published 1896. With it he restored to the world a different view of the Greek goddess of love. No longer was she solely a sexually attractive woman and sponsor of romantic love; Louys reintroduced to the world the ecstatic aspects of her cult and added undertones of perversity and fetish to her image.

The novel concerns a courtesan called Chrysis and her life in the market for pleasure of the classical world. She is originally from Galilee; she is nearly twenty in the story and has been in Alexandria for the last eight years. She works as a courtesan, but her sexual preferences are lesbian (as is the case with many of Louys' female characters). We learn in chapter one that "Greek harlots [had] taught her strange caresses which surprised her at first, but afterwards enchanted her so much that she could not do without them for a whole day."

Chrysis describes her teens in these terms:

> "All who have desired me have had their pleasure with me: men, young men, old men, children, women, young girls. I have refused nobody, do you understand? For seven years... I have only slept alone three nights. Count how many lovers that makes. Two thousand five hundred and more. I do not include those that came in the daytime. Last year I danced naked before twenty thousand persons..."

* * *

In Louys' vision of this ancient world, sensuality and the beauty of the human nude are worshipped. Louys offers what he claims to be an honest and unexpurgated representation of Greek culture, one which is full of dancing girls, juvenile nudity and hints of lesbianism. He got away with this eroticism by distancing himself from his material. By locating his narrative in a far-off land and time, he could pass it off as a historical account, neither endorsing nor rejecting the Egyptians' pagan excesses.

It is very clear from other works by Louys that he regarded Aphrodite as the goddess of wanton or uninhibited sex. In his *Dialogue at Sunset*, a young shepherd proposes premarital sex to a Greek peasant girl, calling her "sister of Aphrodite, girl of clustering hair, like massed grapes." She rejects this, saying

"I should be ashamed to act like [those] who did not wait for their wedding day to learn the secrets of Aphrodite." In another story, *A New Sensation,* the nymph Calisto describes how "the great burning soul of Aphrodite inspired the bodies of lovers and each day a new pleasure – a new pleasure, do you hear? – came down from blue Olympus into the wide beds filled with their enamoured cries."[3]

* * *

Central to Louys' story of Chrysis is the sculptor called Demetrios. At the beginning of the novel, he is the lover of the young Egyptian queen Berenice, a descendant of Astarte-Aphrodite. She commands him to carve a statue of herself in the guise of the goddess, which is to be placed in the city's temple and adored. Demetrios does as she commands, and the result attracts universal acclaim, but he is changed by it:

> "The highest realisation of the queen's beauty, all the idealism it was possible to read into the supple lines of her body, Demetrios had evoked it all from the marble, and from that day onward he imagined that no other woman on earth would ever attain to the level of his dream. His statue became the object of his passion. He adored it only, and madly divorced from the flesh the supreme idea of the goddess, all the more immaterial because he had attached it to life."

Demetrios tires of the queen because she cannot compete with the perfect image of her that he has created and which has become the actual embodiment of the goddess herself:

> "the goddess stood imbued with life upon a pedestal of rose-coloured stone, laden with rich votive offerings. She was

---
3 Both published in the collection *Sanguines.*

naked and fully sexed, tinted vaguely and like a woman. In one hand she held her mirror, the handle of which was a phallus, and with the other she adorned her beauty with a pearl necklace of seven strings. A pearl larger than the others, long and silvery, gleamed between her two breasts, like the moon's crescent between two round clouds."

From this point on, when Demetrios desires a woman, he does not visit the queen but goes instead to the garden of the sacred courtesans that surrounds the temple of Aphrodite. The sex there is free of the demands of a relationship.

The temple of Aphrodite dominates Louys' version of the city of Alexandria, both physically and spiritually. In reality, whilst there is good evidence for very active worship of, and devotion to, Aphrodite in later Egyptian culture (for example, huge myrtle wreaths were paraded through the city at the festival of Ptolemaia), the shrine for which the port city was famed was that of Serapis. Nonetheless, Louys imagines Aphrodite's temple extremely vividly:

"The temple of Aphrodite-Astarte stood outside the gates of the town, in an immense park, full of flowers and shade. The Nile water, conveyed by seven aqueducts, induced an extraordinary verdure all the year round...

The gardens were more than a valley, more than a country; they were a complete world enclosed by bounds of stone and governed by a goddess, the soul and centre of this universe. All around it stood a circular terrace, eighty stades long and thirty-two feet high. This was not a wall; it was a colossal perimeter composed of fourteen hundred houses. A corresponding number of prostitutes inhabited this sacred town, and in this unique spot were represented seventy different nationalities..."

These sacred prostitutes come from every nation of the known world: Louys lists Mysians and Israelites, Phrygians and Cretans, daughters of Ecbatana and Babylon, women from India and even further into South East Asia, Sarmatians, Scythians, Germans, Gauls, Iberians, Numidians, Carthaginians and Negresses – all with their characteristic looks, clothes and ways of making love. What's more:

> "Each woman had brought a little idol of the goddess from her native country, and each adored it in her own tongue, as it stood upon the altar, without understanding the other women. Lakshmi, Ashtaroth, Venus, Ishtar, Freia, Mylitta, Cypris, such were the religious names of their deified pleasure. Some venerated her under a symbolic form: a red pebble, a conical stone, a great knotted shell. Most of them had a little statuette on a pedestal of green wood, usually a rudely-carved figure with thin arms, heavy breasts, and excessive hips. The hand pointed to the delta-shaped locks of the belly. They laid a myrtle-branch at its feet, scattered the altar with rose leaves, and burned a little grain of incense for every prayer granted. It was the confidant of all their troubles, the witness of all their undertakings, the supposed cause of all their pleasures. At their death, it was placed in their fragile little coffin, to watch over their tombs."

We have already seen the importance of roses and incense in the worship of the goddess. We shall return in a little while to the significance of the myrtle offered to her. We know too that scallop shells symbolised her; at Paphos, on Cyprus, a large conical stone, called a *baetyl*, represented Aphrodite in her shrine. The roughly carved statuettes Louys describes may well put us in mind of the prehistoric figurines, carved from ivory, the so-called Venus of Willendorf and others – although these are between ten and thirty thousand years old. His key message in this passage, though, is that reverence for Aphrodite is global.

* * *

In one chapter of *Aphrodite*, Louys imagines and reconstructs the worship of the goddess at her Alexandrian shrine, with offerings being made for her favour and help. The various worshippers dedicate their gifts – flowers, fabrics and jewellery – to different aspects of Aphrodite: Cypris, Goddess of the Fair Crown, Victorious, Chryseia, Cytheraea, Paphia and Epistrophia (the changer of hearts).

Amongst those approaching Aphrodite are two young flute players from Ephesus, girls called Rhodis and Myrtocleia; they are lovers and they ask the Double Goddess of Amathos "if it be true that the tender Adonis is not alone sufficient for you and that sometimes your sleep is retarded by a yet sweeter embrace?" They are followed to the altar by a very young courtesan who offers Aphrodite *Peribasia* (the 'straddling' one) her virginity, symbolised by her blood-stained tunic: "I have dedicated myself to thee since last night." Lastly comes a blushing little child who says:

> "I am not rich enough to give you silver coins, O glittering Olympian goddess. Besides, what could I give you that you lack? Here are flowers, yellow and green, pleated into a wreath for thy feet. And now…" She unbuckled the clasps of her tunic; the tissue slipped down to the ground and she stood revealed quite naked… "I dedicate myself to you, body and soul, Beloved goddess. I desire to enter your gardens and die a courtesan of the temple. I swear to desire naught but love, I swear to love but to love, I renounce the world and I shut myself up in you…"

This little girl's commitment is a life-time one, for "when once a woman had entered the garden, she never left it till the first day of her old age. She gave the half of her gains to the temple, and the remainder went to defray the cost of her meals and perfumes." Louys goes on to describe the courtesans' position and their way of life within the temple complex, the structure and ceremonies of which he reconstructs in vivid and convincing detail:

> "They were not slaves, and each was the real owner of one of the houses of the terrace; but all were not equally beloved, and the most fortunate often found the opportunity of buying the neighbouring houses, which their owners were willing to sell in order to escape the ravages of hunger. These girls carried off their obscene statuettes to the park and searched out a flat stone to serve as an altar, in a corner which henceforth they did not leave. The poorer tradesmen were aware of this. and preferred to address themselves to the women who slept thus in the open air upon the moss near their sanctuaries; but occasionally even these suitors were not forthcoming, and then the poor creatures took to themselves a partner in distress. These passionate friendships developed almost into conjugal love. The couple shared everything down to the last scrap of wool. They consoled one another for their long periods of chastity by alternate complaisances.
>
> Those who had no female friends offered themselves of their own accord as slaves to their more prosperous colleagues. The latter were forbidden to have more than a dozen of these poor creatures in their service, but twenty-two courtesans were quoted as having attained the maximum. These had chosen a motley staff of domestics from all the nationalities.

If, in the course of their stray amours, they conceived a son, he was brought up in the temple-enclosure in the contemplation of the perfect form and in the service of its divinity. If they were brought to bed of a daughter, the child was consecrated to the goddess.

On the first day of its life, they celebrated its symbolic marriage with the son of Dionysos, and the Hierophant deflowered it herself with a little golden knife; for virginity is displeasing to Aphrodite. Later on, the little girl entered the Didascalion, a great monumental school situated behind the temple, and where the theory and practice of all the erotic arts were taught in seven stages: the use of the eyes, the embrace, the motions of the body, the secrets of the bite, of the kiss, and of glottis [which is, I assume, oral sex].

The pupil chose the day of her first experiment at her own good pleasure, because desire is ordained by the goddess, whose will must be obeyed. On that day, she was allotted one of the houses of the terrace, and some of these children, who were not even nubile, counted amongst the most zealous and the most esteemed.

The interior of the Didascalion, the seven class-rooms, the little theatre, and the peristyle of the court, were decorated with ninety-two frescoes designed to sum up the whole of amatory teaching. It was the life-work of one man. Cleochares of Alexandria, the natural son and disciple of Apelles, had terminated them on the eve of his death. Recently, Queen Berenice, who was greatly interested in the celebrated school and sent her young sisters to it, had ordered a series of marble groups from Demetrios in order to complete the decoration; but as yet only one of them had been erected, in the children's class-room.

At the end of each year, in the presence of the entire body of courtesans, a great competition took place, which excited an extraordinary emulation amongst this crowd of women, for the twelve prizes which were offered conferred the right to the most exalted glory it was possible to dream of: the right to enter the Cotytteion.

This last monument was shrouded in so much mystery, that it is impossible for us to give a detailed description of it. We know merely that it was comprised in the peribola and that it had the form of a triangle of which the base was a temple of the goddess Cotytto, in whose name fearful unknown debauches took place. The other two sides of the monument were composed of eighteen houses; they were inhabited by thirty-six courtesans, so sought after by rich lovers that they did not give themselves for less than two minæ: they were the 'baptes' [bathers] of Alexandria. Once a month, at full moon, they assembled in the temple enclosure, maddened by aphrodisiacs, and girt with the canonical phallos. The oldest of the thirty-six was required to take a mortal dose of the terrible erotogenous philtre. The certainty of a speedy death impelled her to attempt without hesitation all the dangerous feats of sensual passion before which the living recoil. Her body, covered with foam, became the centre and model of the whirling orgy; in the midst of prolonged shriekings, cries, tears, and dances, the other naked women embraced her with frenzy, bathed their hair in her sweat, fastened on her burning flesh, and drew fresh ardours from the uninterrupted spasm of this furious agony. Three years these women lived thus – and such was the wild madness of their end at the close of the thirty-sixth month.

Other less venerated sanctuaries had been erected by the women, in honour of the other names of the multiform Aphrodite. There was an altar sacred to the Ouranian Aphrodite, which received the chaste vows of sentimental courtesans: another to the Apostrophian Aphrodite, who granted forgetfulness of unrequited loves; another to the Chrysean Aphrodite, who attracted rich lovers; another to Genetyllis, the patron goddess of women in child-birth; another to Aphrodite of Colias [from Kolias in Attica], who presided over gross passions, for everything which related to love fell within the pious cult of the goddess. But these special altars possessed no efficacy or virtue except in the case of unimportant desires. Their service was haphazard, their favours were a matter of daily occurrence, and their votaries were on terms of familiarity with them. Suppliants whose prayers had been granted made simple offerings of flowers; those who were not content defiled them with their excrements. They were neither consecrated nor kept up by the priests, and their profanation incurred no punishment. Far different was the discipline of the Temple.

The temple, the Great Temple of the Great Goddess, the most sacred spot in all Egypt, the inviolable Astarteïon, was a colossal edifice one hundred and thirty-six feet in length, standing on the summit of the gardens and approached on all sides by seventeen steps. The golden gates were guarded by twelve hermaphrodite hierodules, symbolising the two objects of love and the twelve hours of the night."

In his penultimate paragraph, Louys adds some more epithets or surnames for the goddess to those we have already encountered. Many of these labels simply related to the location of a particular shrine; some were descriptive, such as the Aphrodite *Ambologera* who delayed old age. The Venus *Acidalia* might be both: it might refer to the well at Acidalius where Aphrodite bathed with the three graces, or it might be related to the word *akides*, meaning 'cares' or 'troubles.'

* * *

In Louys' novel, the young sculptor Demetrios one night takes one of his regular walks through the temple grounds, strolling along the terrace where the sacred courtesans await their clients, displaying themselves to the passers-by. He "passed slowly before them and did not weary of admiring. He had never been able to see, without intense emotion, the nakedness of a woman. He understood neither disgust before dead youth nor insensibility before very young girls. Any woman, this evening, could have charmed him."

It is now that we meet one of these temple prostitutes, a girl of ten and a half called Melitta. Her mother is one of the less successful courtesans, who has gone to live in the open air in the temple gardens, whilst her daughter is just starting her career in the service of the goddess. Her age may shock readers (and doubtless this was partly Louys' aim) but it's worth remarking that, in ancient Rome, girls were considered marriageable at twelve and were adult women at fourteen, so that in classical terms this may not, in fact, have been exceptional. Equally, Louys wanted to present his readers with an utterly alien culture, where none of our preconceptions applied. He wished to challenge us profoundly with unfamiliar attitudes to sex, sexuality and religious devotion.[4]

Melitta may still seem very young, but in Louys' imaginative world, sexual maturity and desire come very early. The younger sister of Queen Berenice is Cleopatra.

> "She was then twelve years of age, and no one could tell what her beauty would be. Her body, tall and thin, seemed out of place in a family where all the females were plump. She was ripening like some badly-grafted, bastard fruit of foreign, obscure origin. Some of her lineaments were hard

---

[4] Louys' novel, *Les aventures du roi Pausole*, is also set in an imaginary contemporary kingdom where morals and customs are quite different to our own. Polygamy, polyandry and public nudity prevail.

and bold, as seen in Macedonia; other traits appeared as if inherited from the depths of Nubia, where womankind is tender and swarthy, for her mother had been a female of inferior race whose pedigree was doubtful. It was surprising to see Cleopatra's lips, almost thick, under an aquiline nose of rather delicate shape. Her young breasts, very round, small, and widely separated, were crowned with swelling aureolae, thereby showing she was a daughter of the Nile."

We learn that the princess already has a lover, whom she visits three times daily for sex. It transpires that he is a caged prisoner who has no choice but to submit to her demands. Louys' Alexandria, the exotic and alien capital of a decadent and doomed Egypt, can be a cruel and perverted place.[5]

* * *

Returning to the temple garden, the various prostitutes call out their names to draw his gaze as Demetrios strolls past admiringly, but Melitta attracts his attention more modestly: "a little girl all dressed in blue leaned her head upon her shoulders and said to him, softly, without rising: 'Is there no way?'"

Charmed by her approach, Demetrios chooses Melitta, although he is still surprised to discover how little a girl she is when she slips off her dress and sits on his knee:

> "completely naked [for], when divested of her ample robe, her little body was seen to be so young, so childish of breast, so narrow at the hips, so visibly immature, that Demetrios felt a sense of pity, like a horseman on the point of throwing his man's weight on a delicate young filly."

---

5 Another of Louys' young lovers is ten-year-old prostitute Lili in *Trois filles et leur mère*, whilst all the girls in his *Pybrac* and *Handbook for Young Girls* are sexually active and experienced in the fullest range of practices. In the latter, he declares that all girls should lose their virginity by the age of eight.

He objects that she is not a woman, but Melitta persuades him to stay, protesting that she is nearly eleven. Moreover, she is in the final year at the temple school, although she complains that she is tired of the classes now: "They make you recommence the same lesson twenty times! Things perfectly useless that men never ask for. And then one is tired out, all for nothing."

Melitta admits to already having taken many lovers in honour of Aphrodite, but (ironically, given her own extreme youth) she expresses her dissatisfaction that:

> "They are all too old: it is inevitable. Young men are so foolish! They only like women forty years old. Now and again, I see young men pretty as Eros pass by, and if you were to see what they choose! Hippopotami! It is enough to make one turn pale. I hope sincerely that I shall never reach these women's age: I should be too ashamed to undress. I am so glad to be still quite young. The breasts always develop too soon. I think that the first month I see my blood flow I shall feel ready to die."

She then demonstrates to Demetrios the skills in lovemaking that she has learned for Aphrodite in the temple school:

> "Here the conversation took a less serious if not a more silent turn, and Demetrios rapidly perceived that his scruples were beside the mark in the case of so expert a young lady. She seemed to realise that she was somewhat meagre pasturage for a young man's appetite, and she battled her lover by a prodigious activity of furtive finger-touches, which he could neither foresee nor elude, nor direct, and which never left him the leisure for a loving embrace. She multiplied her agile, firm little body around him, offered herself, refused herself, slipped and turned and struggled. Finally, they grasped one another. But this half hour was merely a long game."

Demetrios, it transpires, is not the only one who enjoys the pleasures of Melitta's young body and the delightful tricks and accomplishments she has learned to bring joy in the goddess' name. She too knows Chrysis. The latter visited her once with a male partner; another time she came by herself to enjoy the little girl alone, and she has promised to return a third time. Such lesbian relationships in ancient Egypt were unremarkable: women often lived together as partners just like married heterosexual couples.[6]

Chrysis, as suggested already, seems to have many female lovers (including both the Ephesian girls Rhodis and Myrtocleia), but she consents to become Demetrios' lover on the condition that he will bring her three precious gifts: a famous courtesan's mirror, the comb worn in her hair by the High Priest's wife and the seven-row necklace of pearls worn by the sculptor's own statue of the goddess in the temple. This will involve considerable risk, including burglary and evading the hermaphrodite guards of the temple sanctuary, but in his obsessive passion for Chrysis, Demetrios agrees to do this, murdering the High Priest's wife in the process.

To secure the items she desires, Chrysis makes her own offerings to Aphrodite in her temple. She presents these to the goddess in her various guises – offering her mirror to:

> "Astarte of the Night, who joins hand to hand and lip to lip … It has seen the haggard darkness of the eyelids and the glitter of the eyes after love, the hair glued to the temples by the sweat of thy battles, O! warrior-queen of ruthless hand, you who joins body to body and mouth to mouth."

Anadyomene receives the courtesan's comb, which "has plunged into her hair tossed by thy convulsions, O furiously-panting mistress of Adonis, that furrows the camber of the loins and

---

[6] R. Antelme & S. Rossini, *Sacred Sexuality in Ancient Egypt,* 2001, 145–148.

racks the stiffening knee!" Lastly, Chrysis gives her necklace to the goddess as "*Hetaira* [prostitute], who drives away the blushes of shamefaced maidens and prompts the lewd laugh, for whom we sell the love that streams from our entrails…"

At the conclusion of the novel, Chrysis displays herself to the populace on the famous Pharos of Alexandria, naked except for the stolen mirror, comb and pearls. A large crowd has gathered, shocked and enraged by the violation of Aphrodite's temple by murder and theft (and another layer of offence is likely to have arisen from the fact that the Pharos was dedicated to Isis-Aphrodite). Chrysis is immediately arrested and is condemned to death, but Demetrios gives her immortality through another statue.

Because of her violation of Aphrodite's sanctuary, Chrysis is denied a proper funeral, and it falls to her occasional lovers, Rhodis and Myrtocleia, to make the necessary arrangements. In fact, the young girls even have to remove her body from the prison and secretly inter her, a final symbol of their regard. This couple have very important roles to perform in Louys' story but, I think, they are intended to have a symbolic function too. A little earlier, I quoted Louys' reference to the temple prostitutes offering myrtle branches to their statuettes of the goddess. Along with the red rose, myrtle is one of the plants especially associated with – and sacred to – Aphrodite. Garlands of the two were often carried in processions or offered at altars; on their wedding days brides wore a myrtle crown and bathed in myrtle scented water.

* * *

It can hardly be coincidence that one of the two Ephesians is named Myrtocleia, a named that perhaps translates as 'closed myrtle.' What Louys might have been trying to imply here may be revealed by a conversation between the two girls that takes place early in the book. Returning home from a party at which they have performed, they discuss their love for each other. Myrtocleia praises her partner's beauty – she is a little nymph, with lovely pale skin, blonde hair and tender breasts:

> "By the girdle of Aphrodite, on which are embroidered all desires, all desires are strangers to me since you are more than my dream … Oh, Rhodis, you know, my singular virginity is like the lips of Pan eating a spring of myrtle; yours is as rosy and pretty as the mouth of a little child."

Here we have both of the goddess' sacred flowers invoked at once in one vivid and intimate compliment. Myrtocleia seems to be named for the goddess *and* for her dark pudenda, Rhodis (*ródo* – rose) for her pinkness. Alternatively, Louys may have had in mind the Greek *rodí,* meaning a pomegranate, another fruit regarded as sacred to and symbolic of Aphrodite; it was the only thing she planted on Cyprus, allegedly. It symbolised blood and sex and had been dedicated to her from the earliest times on the island; hence Clark Ashton Smith's lines: "caressed the vermillion blossoms of the pomegranate/ Whose red is the red of the lips of Astarte." The Latin slang for the female gentials was *myrtus,* just to hammer the point home (as it were). In a sense, then, every time these girls make love together, it is an act of worship of the goddess.[7]

Myrtle, in fact, is never far from Aphrodite. It seems that it was felt suitable for her because of its fragrance, and because it grows on the sea-shore. Latin poet Ovid tells us that, when she first came ashore on Cyprus:

> "Naked, she was drying on the shore her oozy locks, when the satyrs, a wanton crew, espied the goddess. She

---

[7] Clark Ashton Smith, 'Psalm,' from *Ebony & Crystal,* 1922; see too Robert Graves, *The White Goddess,* 371 footnote 1.

perceived it, and screened her body by myrtle interposed: that done, she was safe, and she bids you do the same."[8]

As an evergreen shrub, it's very likely too that myrtle was associated with Aphrodite's role in growth and rebirth. For all these reasons, the goddess bore titles such as *Myrto, Myrtea* and *Myrtoessa*. In Rome, Venus was known as *Cluacina*, she who purifies with myrtle, although later there was some unfortunate confusion over the title, which was transmuted into *Cloacina*, goddess of the sewers....[9]

We see myrtle in many classical sculptures and, later, in paintings by Sandro Botticelli. In his *Venus and Mars*, the lovers recline in front a thicket of myrtle bushes; in the *Birth of Venus*, the attendant awaiting the goddess on the shore of Cyprus has a girdle of roses and a necklace of twined myrtle branches. For that matter, Athena, in Botticelli's *Pallas and the Centaur*, is twined about her bodice and arms with the plant. Discussing sacred sex earlier, readers may recall the story of king Cinyras of Cyprus, who prostituted his daughters for the deity. In one version of his life, one of these girls, Myrrha, offended Aphrodite and was cursed by her to be seized by a passion for her father. However, just as the two were about to engage in incest, the goddess felt pity for her victim and saved her by changing her into a myrtle tree.

It remains to be added that most of the names Louys chose for his characters seem to have been intended to be significant or symbolic. Chrysis means 'gold' in Greek, reflecting her hair colour, but it is also a title for Aphrodite, the golden one; Melitta derives from *méli*, meaning honey. After they have had sex, the little girl demonstrates a further little trick that she has learned in the temple school, smearing honey on her lips and kissing

---

[8] Ovid, *Fasti*, April 1st.
[9] In the *White Goddess*, 394–395, Robert Graves indulges in a rather tenuous argument in which he connects Mary, Star of the Sea, to mermaids, to myrtle and thence to Aphrodite.

Demetrios. Aphrodite was sometimes depicted with a beehive or with honeycomb, representing the sweetness and the stings of love.[10] The young courtesan's name also has the sense of 'balm,' perhaps indicative of the beneficial effect that intercourse with her may have on her older clients. In the next section, we shall discuss Louys' *Songs of Bilitis*, in which we shall meet a young girl called Glottis, with whom the heroine Bilitis considers an affair. Glottis means 'tongue,' which may refer to the fact that she is a singer, or which may have a more sexual connotation, as when Bilitis kisses her girlfriend and "she united her lips with mine and our tongues touched each other." This singer's sister's name, *Kyse*, means 'kiss,' leaving the erotic undertones in very little doubt.[11]

* * *

Louys' recreation of the temple of Aphrodite and its rites reads, in places, like an archaeological report. It is, though, largely a work of fantasy that embodies his deepest sexual fascinations. His other books, especially those manuscripts published after his death in 1925 (*Pybrac, Trois filles de leur mère* and *The Handbook for Young Girls*), disclose an obsession with anal sex, incest, lesbianism and dildoes – preferably all four at once. In light of these later works, it is hardly surprising that he depicted the goddess and her cult in the manner in which he did. As Louys wrote, "desire is ordained by the goddess" and it seems that all sexual pleasure was sanctified, whatever its form, whoever its participants. Rhodis and her girlfriend Myrtocleia seek reassurance that their passion is blessed by Aphrodite and, in Louys' reconstruction of the goddess' worship, there seems little question that this was the case. The less successful courtesans form relationships with other women; the sacred prostitutes

---

10 See some of the paintings by Cranach, mentioned at the start of this chapter, for examples.
11 *Bilitis*, Song 52.

accept clients whatever their sex (or age) and, as the author imagined so vividly, the fatal rite of Cotytto (more properly, *Kotys*, a Thracian goddess) involved courtesans wearing strap-on dildoes penetrating the doomed woman in an ecstatic drug fuelled orgy – "attempting without hesitation all the dangerous feats of sensual passion before which the living recoil."

Louys' approach to sexuality was liberated and non-judgmental, as will be seen in his *Songs of Bilitis*, which concerns the lesbian love life of Bilitis and which presents same-sex marriage as a fact of the classical Greek world (which it almost certainly was not). Likewise, his *Aventures du Roi Pausole* imagine a society where, again, same-sex relationships, polygamy and polyandry and public nudity are all unremarkable features of society in an invented kingdom. We might suggest, therefore, that *Aphrodite* and her worship represent another aspect of the author's ideal world. Love – and pleasure – should be treated as sacred and Louys is unwilling to place any limits at all upon the expression of desire.

The Songs of Bilitis

Louys published *Les Chansons de Bilitis* in 1894. Like *Aphrodite*, the songs are set in the Hellenic world and are in touch with historical reality without being truly authentic. Bilitis is a courtesan and poet; she is alleged to have been a friend of Sappho and to have been an inspiration to later poets, some of whom plagiarised her work. Her 'Songs' purport to have been recovered from her tomb and give an account of her life and her love affairs.

The book's abiding fame derives from the fact that it presents itself as an honest record of passions and sex life of a lesbian living in the sixth century BCE. Rather like Chrysis in the previous book, Bilitis as a girl is attracted to men, but a night spent sharing a bed with her friend Selenis opens her eyes to sex with another female. Selenis pretends to be Lykas, a shepherd boy Bilitis likes: "She slipped her leg over mine to caress me gently… And tenderly, in the silence, she enchanted my reverie into a singular illusion." A more general same-sex attraction, and a willingness to be fluid in gender roles, is indicated by this song:

> "Upon the soft grass, in the night, the young girls with hair of violets have all danced together, one of each pair playing the part of the lover.
>
> The virgins said: "We are not for you." And as if they were ashamed, they hid their virginity. A satyr played upon the flute under the trees.
>
> The others said: "We have come to seek you." They arranged their tunics about them like the dress of men; and they struggled in ecstasy while entwining their dancing legs.
>
> Then each one, feeling herself vanquished, took her lover by the ears even as one takes a beaker by the two handles, and, the head bent forward, drank a kiss."[12]

Having left behind her home – and a child – and travelled to the island of Mytilene, Bilitis considers an affair with one or other of two young dancers, Glottis and Kyse, who offer to teach her "the honey of a woman's caresses." She is torn between the two little girls, who sit either side of her holding her hands and caressing her breasts, not knowing which to kiss and take to bed and which to reject. Kyse is an especially enticing prospect, skipping around energetically before dissolving in laughter, grabbing her sister's breasts, biting her shoulder and throwing her to the floor, "like a goat which wishes to play." However, Bilitis very soon afterwards meets the girl who is to be the love of her life, Mnasidika.

---

12 *Bilitis*, Songs 25 & 16.

As well as bringing same-sex love to the fore, rather than it forming part of the backdrop to the character's lives – as in *Aphrodite* – the worship of that deity as the goddess of love is addressed much more consistently in the *Songs of Bilitis*. Needless to say, this Aphrodite smiles on all lovers, whatever their sexualities. In fact, in his pseudo-academic introduction to the book, Louys restated the sacred status of prostitutes that formed one theme of the previous novel:

> "... love was considered holy among the peoples of antiquity. The courtesans of Amathus [one of the goddess' shrines] were not, like ours, lost creatures, exiled from all worldly society; they were girls from the best families of the city. Aphrodite had given them beauty and they thanked the goddess by consecrating to the service of her worship the beauty they had received. All the cities, like those of Kypros, which possessed a temple rich in courtesans, regarded those women with careful respect."

When Bilitis meets Mnasidika, in a field, under a bush of myrtle, it is love at first sight for both of them. A sign that they're made for each other seems to be that they both wear a similar necklace, as Mnasidika says:

> "I'll carry nothing with me but the little nude Astarte which is hanging from my necklace. We'll place it close to yours, and reward them with red roses every night."
>
> "The little guardian Astarte which protects Mnasidika, was modelled at Camiros by a very clever potter. She is as large as your thumb, of fine-ground yellow clay. Her tresses fall and circle about her narrow shoulders. Her eyes are cut quite widely and her mouth is very small. For she is the All-Beautiful. Her right hand indicates her delta, which is peppered with tiny holes about her lower belly and along her groins. For she is the All-Lovable. Her left

hand supports her round and heavy breasts. Between her spreading hips swings a large and fertile belly. For she is the Mother of All."[13]

Louys includes a hymn to Astarte in which she and Aphrodite seem compounded:

"Mother inexhaustible and incorruptible, creator, first-born, engendered by thyself and by thyself conceived, issue of thyself alone and seeking joy within thyself, Astarte!

Oh! perpetually fertile, virgin and nurse of all that is, chaste and lascivious, pure and revelling, ineffable, nocturnal, sweet, breather of fire, foam of the sea!

Thou who grants favours in secret, thou who unites, thou who loves, thou who possessed with furious desire the multiplied races of savage beasts and couples the sexes in the wood.

Oh, irresistible Astarte! hear me, take me, possess me, oh, Moon! and thirteen times each year draw from my womb the sweet libation of my blood!"

Bearing in mind Melitta in *Aphrodite,* and the aforementioned dancing girls Glottis and Kyse, with their childish little bellies, it is worthwhile emphasising that Mnasidika too is not very old. She is still living at home with her mother when the pair meet. She brings her toys with her when they start to live together and Bilitis (who calls her Little Sister) gives her a doll to play with, which she does, pretending it is their child, cradling and breast feeding it before it is placed in its cradle to sleep. Mnasidika plays with her lover in a similar way, dressing her hair in a variety of ways before pretending to breast feed at her bosom.[14]

A physical and emotional passion develops between the two. As Bilitis says: "I feel myself bitten by voracious Aphrodite."

---
13 *Bilitis*, Songs 50 & 51.
14 Sons 60 & 62.

Sadly, their love eventually wanes and Bilitis is deserted. She moves away to Cyprus (Aphrodite's island) to escape her painful loss and her memories.[15]

Throughout the book we see Bilitis and others making offerings to Aphrodite. As a young girl, she prays for love, hanging a garland of roses on a tree "for Aphrodite, whom I adore in my heart, for she only can give me what my lips most need." Further offerings are made by her to *Kypris Victorious* after she loses her virginity with Lykas, to seek protection for Mnasidika from Laughter Loving Aphrodite (two hares and two doves) and to try to prolong Mnasidika's love.[16] Bilitis also describes some of the ecstatic ceremonies performed for the divine lovers, Dionysus and Aphrodite:

> "Through the forests that overhang the sea, the Maenads madly rushed. Maskale, with the hot breasts, howled and brandished the sycamore phallos, smeared with red. All leaped and ran and cried aloud beneath their robes and crowns of twisted vine, crotals clacking in their hands, and thyrses splitting the bursting skins of echoing dulcimers. With sopping hair and agile limbs, breasts reddened and tossed about, sweat of cheeks and foam of lips, oh, Dionysos! they offered in return the love that you had poured in them. And the sea-wind tossed Heliokomis' russet hair unto the sky, and whipped it into a furious flame on her body's white-wax torch."

> "I had crouched on the edge of the highest promontory. The sea was black as a field of violets. And the Milky Way was gushing from the great divine breast. About me a thousand Maenads slept in the torn-up flowers, long grasses mingled with their flowing hair, and now the sun was born from the eastern waters. These the same waves and these the self-

---
15 Song 68.
16 *Bilitis,* Songs 24, 35, 36, 57, 90.

same shores that saw one day the white body of Aphrodite rising… I suddenly hid my eyes in my hands, for I had seen the water trembling with a thousand little lips of light: the pure sex, or it may have been the smile of *Kypris Philommeïdes* (Aphrodite the Laughter Loving)."

"Astarte's priestesses engage in love at the rising of the moon; then they arise and bathe themselves in a great basin with a silver rim. With crooked fingers they comb their tangled locks, and their purple-tinted hands twined in their jet-black curls are like so many coral-branches in a dark and running sea. They never pluck their pubic hair, for the goddess's triangle marks their bellies as a temple; but they tint themselves with paint-brush, and heavily scent themselves. Astarte's priestesses engage in love at the setting of the moon, then in a carpeted hall where burns a high gold lamp they stretch themselves at random."

"In the thrice mysterious enclosure where men have never entered, we have fêted you, Astarte of the Night. Mother of the World, Well-Spring of the life of all the Gods! I shall reveal a portion of the rite, but no more of it than is permitted. About a crowned Phallus, a hundred and twenty women swayed and cried. The initiates were dressed as men, the others in the split tunics. The fumes of incense and the smoke of torches floated like clouds around us. I wept burning tears and then, at the feet of Berbeia,[17] we threw all ourselves down, stretched on our backs. Then, when the religious act had been consummated, and when into the holy triangle the purpled phallus had been plunged anew, the mysteries began; but I shall say no more.[18]

---

17 Perhaps Louys means *Verbeia*, a mother goddess of Roman West Yorkshire.
18 Songs 64–67.

So far as we can tell, then, Louys imagines a rite as scandalous as anything the ancient historians hinted at so disapprovingly. Worked into a frenzy by wine and dance, the worshippers all have sex in turn with a woman wearing a wooden dildo, perhaps in a manner suited to the gender they have assumed for the ritual. If so, this would be entirely appropriate to the goddess. This seems even more the case when we learn that the title employed by Louys, *Kypris Philommeïdes*, had a near homophone, *Philommedes*, which meant 'Lover of Genitals.'

Working as a prostitute and brothel keeper on Cyprus, Bilitis and her girls have to perform erotic dances to entertain audiences at banquets and festivals. For example, "Nephele of the glossy armpits will imitate the love of doves between her rosy breasts. A singer in a broidered peplos will sing the songs of Rhodes, accompanied by flute-blowers with myrtle-garlands twined about their chestnut limbs." She sees all these performances as dedicated to the goddess of love:

> "You ask, oh, Bilitis, why have I become a Lesbian? But what flute-player is not lesbian a little? I am poor; I have no bed; I sleep with her who wishes me, and thank her with whatever charms I have. We danced quite naked when we still were small; you know what dances, oh, my dear: the twelve desires of Aphrodite. We look at one another, compare our nakedness, and find ourselves so pretty. During the long night we become inflamed for the pleasure of the guests; but our ardour is not feigned, and we feel it so much that sometimes one of us entices a willing friend behind the doors. How can we then love men, who are so rough with us? They seize us like whores, and leave us before we reach orgasm. You who are a woman, you know what I feel. You give pleasure to others as you would be pleased yourself."[19]

---

19 *Bilitis*, Songs 119 & 120.

There are further hints of the presence of the goddess in some of Bilitis' descriptions of sex and love:

> "At night, they left us on a high white terrace, fainting among the roses. Warm perspiration flowed like heavy tears from our armpits, running over our breasts. An overwhelming voluptuousness flushed our thrown-back heads. Four captive doves, bathed in four different perfumes, fluttered silently above our heads. Drops of scent fell from their wings upon the naked women. I was streaming with the essence of the iris. Oh, weariness! I laid my cheek upon a young girl's belly, who cooled her body with my moist hair. My open mouth was drunk with her saffron-scented skin. She slowly closed her thighs about my neck."

> "Here lies the delicate body of Lydia, little dove, the happiest of all the courtesans, who, more than all the others, loved orgies, and floating hair, soft dances and hyacinth-coloured tunics. More than all the rest, she adored the mingling of tongues, kisses on the cheek, games to which the lamp alone bore witness, and love which bruises the limbs. And now she is a little shade. But, before she was entombed, her hair was arranged and she was laid in roses; the very slab that covers her is soaked with essences and sweet perfumes."[20]

Birds frequently represent the goddess in the songs; whilst she is still young, Bilitis sings:

> "Sparrow, bird of Kypris, accompany our first desires with your song. The fresh bodies of young girls bloom with flowers, just as blooms the earth. The night of all our dreams arrives and we whisper it together. At times we match our different beauties, our long hair, our budding

---
20 Songs 106 & 118.

breasts, our quail-plump deltas, hidden beneath the newly springing down. Just yesterday I competed this way against Melantho, who's older than me. She was proud of her bosom, which sprouted within the month, and, mocking at my flattened chest, called me Little Child. No man could possibly have seen us, we showed ourselves nude before the other girls, and, if she won upon one point, I vanquished her by far upon the others. Sparrow, bird of the Kyprian, accompany our first desires with your notes."

Later in life, waking from a night of passion, Bilitis sees a dove at her window and asks what month it is. It replies, "It is the month when women are in love." Bilitis had affectionately termed Mnasidika 'Little Dove'; she also compared the girl's breasts to two beautiful doves, as she cradled them in her own hands, or which she would offer to Bilitis to fondle, "as one would offer to the goddess a pair of living turtle doves."[21]

Roses often feature in Bilitis' descriptions, as we've already seen in the description of Lydia's funeral and the aftermath of one orgy. In one song, an unhappy woman is told that "The love of women is the most beautiful of all that mortals know." To cure her depression, she's encouraged to go to see Satyra, daughter of Bilitis' neighbour Gorgo: "her bum is a rose of the sun and she will not refuse you the pleasure that she herself prefers." Less happily, Bilitis also recalls seeing a little rose seller desperate to sell some blossoms to a group of young men: "Buy something from me. Explain yourself, little creature, for we don't know what you're selling: yourself? your roses? or both of them together? If you buy all these flowers, I will give you mine for nothing." The boys bought her and her even younger sister too. "They had no breasts; they did not even know how to smile. They trotted off like kids led to the slaughter."[22]

---

21 *Bilitis* Songs 12, 106, 128, 58, 59 & 65.
22 Songs 118 & 129.

In old age, with death fast approaching, Bilitis addresses Aphrodite as a "merciless goddess" when she realises how her youth and beauty have faded. Nevertheless, within a few lines, she declares "I have shorn all my hair, and twined it in my girdle and I offer it to thee, eternal Kypris! I shall not cease from loving thee. This is the last verse of the pious Bilitis." Readers may recall that we have authentic records of retiring courtesans giving their wigs and hairpieces to the goddess; the act of Bilitis combining the hair with the girdle is, of course, highly symbolic: it is a surrender or renunciation of the life she has lived into the hands of the goddess.

Two epitaphs follow: in one Bilitis affirms that she "adored Astarte at Kypros." In the second we learn that:

> "As a child I was taught the loves of Adonis and Astarte, the mysteries of holy Syria, and death and the return to She-of-the-Rounded-Eyes. If I have been a courtesan, but where was the harm in that? Was this not my work as a woman? The Stranger, the Mother-of-Everything, guides us. She cannot wisely be ignored."[23]

Louys – An Afterword

In the 1890s, Louys began to write a series of short stories based upon classical myths, such as those of Ariadne and Danae. These were published individually before being collected in one volume as *The Twilight of the Nymphs*. One of the first of these, *Leda*, written in 1893, concludes with some thoughts upon mythology and its symbolism. The narrator of the tale tells the women listening to him that "Symbols should never be explained. They should never be penetrated. Have belief. Do not doubt. That which figures as a symbol hides a truth but it is not made manifest for, otherwise, why should it be symbolised?"

---

23 Song 143 & Epitaphs 1 & 2.

Forms conceal the invisible and should not be examined too closely, for then the mystery would be lost. He explains:

> "The undulous reflection in the springs is the essence of the naiad. The buck standing amidst the goats is the essence of the satyr. One or another among you is the essence of Aphrodite."

Each woman can embody some aspect of the spirit of the goddess, whether it is when she is a mother or when she is a lover. This must simply be known and accepted, for "such is the condition of love and happiness."

SADER MASOCH, *VENUS IN FURS*

Venus in Furs (*Venus im Pelz*) is probably the best-known work of the Austrian author Leopold von Sacher-Masoch. The novella was published in 1870, based substantially on Sader-Masoch's own experiences, and addresses issues of female domination and sadomasochism.

The title of the book derives from a painting in the 'Old Master' style which is said to hang in the home of Severin, a friend of the book's narrator. It shows:

> "A beautiful woman with a radiant smile upon her face, with abundant hair tied into a classical knot, on which white powder lay like a soft hoarfrost, was resting on an ottoman, supported on her left arm. She was nude in her dark furs. Her right hand played with a lash, while her bare foot rested carelessly on a man, lying before her like a slave, like a dog. In the sharply outlined, but well-formed lineaments of this man lay brooding melancholy and passionate devotion; he looked up to her with the ecstatic burning eye of a martyr."

THE GODDESS IN PROSE

This imaginary image is, in turn, inspired by Titian's *Venus with a Mirror,* in which the goddess sits admiring her reflection in a glass held by Cupid, her fur-trimmed robe having slipped down about her waist.

Sader-Massoch's narrator has dreams in which he speaks with Venus about love while she sits wrapped in fur (against the cold, rather than with any avowed erotic intent). The dreamer accuses the goddess of unfaithfulness to him as her lover. "You are a divine woman, but nevertheless a woman, and like every woman cruel in love," he tells her. She rejects this: "What you call cruel is simply the element of passion and of natural love, which is woman's nature and makes her give herself where she loves, and makes her love everything that pleases her." For her, love is "only a question of pleasure," whereas her Germanic lover is instilled with guilt over expressing his natural desires, battling with an "always unsatisfied craving for the nudity of paganism." Venus' philosophy for dealing with her male lovers is this:

> "The more cruelly she treats him and the more faithless she is, the worse she uses him, the more wantonly she plays with him, the less pity she shows him, by so much the more will she increase his desire, be loved, worshipped by him."

The narrator describes these troubling dreams to his friend, Severin, who recommends reading a manuscript, *Memoirs of a Suprasensual Man,* as a means of escaping his obsession with cruel women.

This manuscript concerns a man, also called Severin, who is attracted by a widow called Wanda. He describes her as his Venus, comparing her to a stone statue of the goddess in a nearby garden. Severin has become obsessed with this image: "It is sufficient to say that this Venus is beautiful. I love her passionately with a morbid intensity; madly as one can only love a woman who never responds to our love with anything but an eternally uniform, eternally calm, stony smile. I literally adore her." He imagines that the statute comes to life, dressed in fur, and treats him with contempt.

Immediately after this vision of the goddess, Severin meets Wanda. She is an independent woman who was well educated as a girl, claiming that her best friends when she was a child were Venus and Apollo. She tells him: "my principles are very pagan. I will live my own life as it pleases me." She has decided to reject Christian marriage and simply to pursue her own happiness instead. "Shall I belong to one man whom I don't love, merely because I have once loved him? No... I love everyone who pleases me, and give happiness to everyone who loves me... I am young, rich, and beautiful, and I live serenely for the sake of pleasure and enjoyment."

Severin asks to become Wanda's slave and for her to treat him in progressively more degrading ways. Wanda at first neither agrees to – nor understands – his wishes, which are so much at odds with her own philosophy, but she humours him and slowly comes to enjoy her position as mistress, although she despises her slave for his submissiveness. Severin's emotions whilst he is being degraded by her are the 'suprasensuality' of the manuscript's title.

In due course, Wanda meets a Greek man to whom she is prepared to submit herself. Together the pair, as Apollo and Venus, abuse, beat and humiliate Severin until he is finally forced to accept that he must escape from them. At the end of the book, cured of his obsession, Severin concludes that, in the society of the mid-nineteenth century, women could only ever be either slaves or despots over men, but never their companions. Companionship would only be possible when women had equal rights in all aspects of their lives, he realises.

Of course, in 1967, *The Velvet Underground* were inspired by the novella to write the song, *Venus in Furs*. In a trend that we shall see again later in the visual arts, the age of the heroine dropped markedly:

> "Shiny, shiny, shiny boots of leather,
> Whiplash girl-child in the dark…"

In Lou Reed's vision, the dominant mistress is still a juvenile. This cruel junior Venus may have little basis in Sader-Masoch's original work, but she descends, in part at least, from Louÿs' Melitta, combined with a harsher contemporary reality. In 1960s USA sex with underage girls was common enough to merit a colloquial name and, in places like New York, it may well not have been too difficult to find a young goddess to impose her will upon a supplicant, bestowing "love not given lightly."[24]

---

[24] R.E.L. Masters, *The Hidden World of Erotica,* 1973, 366, footnote 2 labels the practice "honey fucking". He glosses this slang phrase in good academic style, albeit in a strange pseudo-Latin, *"coitus cum nymphet"* – *cum puella* would plainly have been strictly correct – if less apt and resonant for the time period.

"Strike Dear Mistress" – Hymns to Venus

Reference to the Velvet Underground highlights the fact that Venus-Aphrodite is a natural subject for popular music. Pop songs continually deal with love, so the goddess of love will never be far away. The sheer number of songs in which Venus or Aphrodite are mentioned as symbols of love and the ideal woman, or in which Venus and Mars (men and women) are contrasted, presented a problem of selection when preparing this book, so only the most famous or relevant artists and songs have been preferred. Even so, divorced from the rhythm and tunes, the lyrics are not always strong, when regarded as poetry, but they do testify to the continuing influence and power of the goddess.

In 1969 Dutch rock band *Shocking Blue* released *Venus*, a song that proved a worldwide hit for them and then for *Bananarama*, who released a cover version in 1986. The lyrics are nothing remarkable:

> "A Goddess on a mountain top
> Was burning like a silver flame
> The summit of beauty and love
> And Venus was her name...
> Well, I'm your Venus
> I'm your fire, what's your desire?"

Shocking Blue's recorded television performance, with vocalist Mariska Veres dressed in black leather, with a good deal of cleavage exposed, laid down a template for pop representations of the goddess (although they may have drawn in turn upon Lou Reed's vision). *Bananarama*'s video featured a red PVC devil catsuit and suggestions of vampirism, making their love goddess a great deal more dangerous to know. In addition, the videos for both songs reflect the fetish connotations that have attached to Venus since the publication of Sader-Massoch's book.

Kylie Minogue's *Aphrodite*, from 1986, is a similarly dangerous lover, who promises to make her partner's heart stop:

> "Oh, I'm fierce and I'm feeling mighty
> I'm a golden girl, I'm an Aphrodite...
> Don't you mess with me, you don't want to fight me...
> Here's what I do
> When I know what I can do –
> I let you in into my world
> With mouth to mouth
> And kiss to kiss..."

Lady Gaga's *Venus*, released in 2013, is an "Aphrodite lady, seashell bikini" from the planet Venus; she invites her potential partner to act sleezy, to "have an oyster, baby, it's Aphrod-isy" then to "blast off to a new dimension (in your bedroom)." She begs the goddess of love, "please take me to your leader," wondering if she's enamoured. Gaga appears to have more than a passing knowledge of the classical mythology, for in G.U.Y. (Girl Under You) she addresses her lover in these terms: "Greetings Himeros/God of sexual desire, son of Aphrodite," and offers to introduce him to exciting new sexual positions.

An unexpected knowledge of the classics might also be ascribed to *Cradle of Filth*, from Hadleigh in Essex, who in the song *Bathory Aria* (1998) sing how:

> "I would have clasped her so tight
> Like storm-beached Aphrodite

Drowned on Kytherean tides
And kissed her –
For from her alone
My lips would have known
Enigmas of shadowy vistas
Where pleasures took flesh
And pain, remorseless
Came freezing the breath
Of raucous life hushed unto whispers."

The same band also reference Astarte in at least two other songs, *The Principle of Evil Made Flesh* and *Lustmord and Wargasm (The Lick of Carnivorous Winds)*. The band also mention Ishtar in numerous tracks, for example *The Black Goddess Rises*, as well as Venus – for instance, in *Beauty Slept in Sodom*. They clearly appreciated the abiding dark power of these age-old stories.

In passing, here, we might also note the track *The Fountain of Salmacis* from the album *Nursery Crymes* by public schoolboys *Genesis* (1971). The track recounts (at length) the story of Hermaphroditus and the nymph.

A darker view of the goddess' power is found in 'The Chemicals' by *Garbage*.

"Aphrodite's siren smiles
She steals anything she likes
Everything you never said
Everything you never did
Everything you fantasised."

It goes without saying that humans will rarely profit from loving divinities, as a quote from the 1999 film *Notting Hill* reminds us:

"*Max*: Let's face facts, this was always a no-win situation. Anna's a goddess: you know what happens to mortals who

get involved with gods.
William: Buggered, is it?
Max: Every time."

Probably predictably, American rock band *Kiss* were not awed by such warnings and took a macho view of the goddess, reducing her to a beauty without her own agency. In *God of Thunder* they declared:

"You've got something about you
You've got something I need
Daughter of Aphrodite
Hear my words and take heed –

I was born on Olympus
To my father a son
I was raised by the demons
Trained to reign as the one

God of thunder and rock and roll
The spell you're under
Will slowly rob you of your virgin soul."

It seems unlikely that the deity who seduced Adonis and Anchises would reckon much to being addressed as a sexual plaything and – in any case – her virgin soul is a thing of the very distant past. Far more appropriate, I suspect, is the power manifested in RuPaul's *Queens Everywhere*, which asserts her independence whilst unconsciously giving a nod back to Arthur Rimbaud and the callipygous deity: "Body of a Goddess, face of Aphrodite/ She's a new bitch, Miss Ass Almighty…"

For Swedish singer Tove Lo (*Bitches*, 2017) the goddess is the pagan Great Mother, representing fertility:

> "Rise high, pollinate, Aphrodite, right
> Turn my touches into neon light
> Chat it up, now, doggy, come suck my eight titties
> I'm a three-headed goddess from the full moon land
> Venus hit the bong, going to sing it straight."

In *Blood Sugar Sex Magik,* the title track of the 1991 album of the same name, the *Red Hot Chili Peppers* also invoked the divinity as goddess of fertility, as well as imagining the transformative effect for a mortal of sleeping with her:

> "Step into a heaven where I keep it on the soul side
> Girl, please me, be my soul bride
> Every woman has a piece of Aphrodite
> Copulate to create a state of sexual light
> Kissing her virginity, my affinity
> I mingle with the gods, I mingle with divinity."

The association of Venus with sexual fluidity lies at the core of Björk's 1993 song, *Venus as a Boy*:

> "His wicked sense of humour
> Suggests exciting sex
> His fingers, they focus on her
> Touches, he's Venus as a boy…
> He believes in a beauty
> He's Venus as a boy."

Aerosmith's *Dude Looks Like a Lady* tackles the same issues, if more uncomfortably, perhaps: "She had the body of a Venus, Lord imagine my surprise."

Arguably one of the most significant modern hymns to Venus-Aphrodite is a song that doesn't explicitly mention her, but which still examines and celebrates the 'polymorphous perversity' of her cult. The track is *Girls and Boys* by Blur, from their 1994 album *Parklife*. The lyrics describe the hedonism of young people enjoying an annual holiday on the sunny beaches of Greece and looking for some summer romance – or, perhaps more strictly, some sex – with:

> "Girls who want boys
> Who like boys to be girls
> Who do boys like they're girls
> Who do girls like they're boys
> Always should be someone you really love."

This fluidity of preference and behaviour lies at the core of the Aphrodisian cult as we have already seen – and has done so for millennia.

She may be thousands of years old, but the iconography of Venus in her scallop shell, floating on the sea and inspiring love in men and women, remains fixed indelibly in our cultural subconscious, still recognisable and resonant.

"Venus in her naked glory" – The Goddess in Art

Artists have always loved classical mythology. The ancient legends provide a wide range of subjects, many of which involve a thrilling mix of violence, sex and nudity. Satyrs cavorting with nymphs, or uninhibited Bacchanalian orgies, offered scenes of intoxicated ecstasy, making abandoned maenads and bassarids especially popular. Venus has always been especially popular because "her naked glory" lies at the heart of her passionate nature and is inseparable from what Marlowe called "Venus' mutual pleasure."[1]

Venus is one of the few classical divinities (and, for that matter, ancient Greek sculptures) who is still immediately recognisable to people the world over. This familiarity in large measure derives from her role, but she is known too because representations of her form part of our subconscious. The Venus de Milo and Sandro Botticelli's *Birth of Venus* are iconographic images. We know them – even if we know nothing else about the goddess that inspired them.

Visual representations of the goddess are, of course, very frequently feature sex and nudity. Hence this little verse form Robert Browning – *A Rhyme for a Child Viewing a Naked Venus in a Painting of 'The Judgment of Paris'*:

---

[1] See, for instance, Lovis Corinth's *Bacchae* and *Bacchanal*. Quotations from Christopher Marlowe, *Hero & Leander,* First Sestiad, line 12 & *Elegia* III.

"He gazed and gazed and gazed and gazed,
Amazed, amazed, amazed, amazed."

FRANCOIS BOUCHER

During the eighteenth century, a particular style of French painting emerged from Rococo which is called *fete* or *peinture galante*. The name indicates its subject matter: it's all about attractive women and love. It's generally felt that the first picture of this new genre was painted by Jean-Antoine Watteau in 1717. The *Voyage to Cythera* (or *Pilgrimage* or *Embarkation*) should more properly be called the 'Departure from Cythera' as it shows a group of lovers in the process of returning to their ship after a visit to the shrine of Venus. The work has a double significance for us: not only did it mark the beginning of a school of painting concerned with love and sex, but its title inspired Charles Baudelaire to write the poem of the same name.

Francois Boucher (1703–1770) was a painter to the court of Louis XV. Perhaps his most famous picture was his portrait of Marie-Louise O'Murphy, a penniless thirteen-year-old beauty with a talent for fellatio. He showed her sprawled wantonly naked on her front on a chaise long, her thighs spread and her pert buttocks presented for our delectation. She seems to revel in her physical charms, awaiting the arrival of a lover. In fact, the picture brought her one. The king saw the painting, expressed a desire to meet the subject to see if she was as attractive in the flesh, and promptly took her as his mistress, even though he was three times her age.

Sexually desirable young females with plump faces and pert breasts were Boucher's speciality. He painted scenes of Venus numerous times, but possibly the most memorable is *Venus Playing with Two Doves,* painted about 1750. The goddess is shown naked, lying on her back on a bed with the two doves clutched passionately to her young bosom. Her legs spread apart, revealing her hairless vulva, and her head lolls back, eyes closed and lips parted, in sensual delight. Most of Boucher's paintings of Venus are nowhere near as erotic as this. His *Birth of Venus, Toilette of Venus* and *Bath of Venus* are just a few of the canvases that exemplify this rather more sedate and demure goddess. She may disport herself with nymphs, cupids and putti, but decorum is preserved and there are always robes and wisps of material at hand to preserve her modesty.

It might, not unreasonably, be supposed that the doves appear in this image for purely sensuous effect. We might well compare numerous paintings by Boucher's contemporary, Jean-Baptiste Greuze, in which winsome young girls clutch various small birds, or kittens, puppies or even lambs, to their bosoms. With Greuze, this not infrequently also involves the accidental bearing of one or both juvenile breasts, heightening the titillating effect: soft, round creatures are held tight against soft, little tits; sometimes the birds have died and there is even a suggestion of attempting to breast feed the poor animals to revive them. Greuze's contemporary Jean Baptiste Fragonard painted a *Young Girl with Two Puppies* (c.1770) in which the subject has slipped her blouse off her shoulders so that she can cradle the two tiny dogs against her bared breasts. His *Young Girl with a Cat* of the same year is very similar, as is *Young Girl with a Dove,* which may be by someone from Fragonard's studio or an imitator: the subject cradles the doves beneath her bare bosom. Both pictures are deliberately arranged to emphasise the girl's physical charms: the girl with the cat wears a thin lace around her neck which falls between and highlights her petite breasts; the model with the dove is posed to look sweetly over one shoulder whilst slightly arching her torso backwards, this has the effect of raising her chest, whilst a blue bow around her neck again subtly draws attention to her bare flesh. Fragonard's *Two Girls Playing with their Dogs* adds a lesbian note, as two juvenile females, dressed only in their shifts, play together on a bed with their two dogs.

Very closely related are the so-called *'Gimblette'* images, painted, for example, by Fragonard, and carved by Clodion, in which a naked girl lies on a bed, dandling a fluffy puppy on her feet. This trend for pictures of young females clutching soft animals persisted into the nineteenth century – its simple suggestiveness plainly making the theme enduringly popular with buyers.[2]

These works are all very consciously erotic and there can be little doubt that titillation was Boucher's primary aim in *Venus Playing with Two Doves*. Nonetheless, he may at the same time not have been unaware of classical precedent. Birds, most especially doves, are sacred to Aphrodite and symbolised the goddess; they pulled her chariot across the heavens (although other stories give this role to sparrows or swans). It seems likely, in fact, that the Greek word for dove, *peristera*, is taken directly from the Phoenician *perah Ishtar*, Ishtar's bird.

As a further note, another highly appealing aspect of the cult of Aphrodite is the fact that it eschewed animal sacrifices – at least in Empedocles' time – and the shedding of blood was entirely prohibited at Paphos. Rather than presenting the goddess the corpses of birds and other small animals, incense, essential oils and opium were burnt for her, small images were presented, and fruit, flowers, honey and other food stuffs were presented – the "amorous herbs and flowers" prepared for the feast of Venus in John Keats' *Lamia*. In the *Homeric Hymn*, for example, the goddess is called "the one with the beautiful garlands." Aphrodite came to be particularly closely associated with perfumes and scents, from both incense and flowers.[3]

Boucher died suddenly in his studio, aged sixty-seven. According to one story, he was in the act of painting Venus' backside; if so, it was arguably a very fitting end. The tastes he

---

[2] Other examples include Fragonard, *Marie Madeleine Colombe Holding A Dove*, Antoine Vestier, *Woman Holding a Dove*, John Rising, *Girl with Dove*, Emile Munier, *Girl Holding a Dove*, Charles Joshua Chaplin's *Young Woman with a Dove* and *A Beauty with Doves* or James Sant, *Love's Messenger*.

[3] Empedocles, *On Nature & Purifications*; Keats, *Lamia*, Part One, line 318.

had catered for remained popular for another couple of decades at least.

Fragonard, just like Boucher, was keenly alive to the wider erotic potential of the Venus-myth. Two pictures, not ostensibly featuring the goddess, still seem to me to take full advantage of her uninhibited sensual power. *The Stolen Shift* of 1765 shows a hovering cupid pulling the blouse off a girl on her bed; it's hard to tell whether the young female is asleep or simply resisting only feebly as she is exposed; there's a healthy flush on her cheeks – and also on her buttocks. *All Ablaze* (*Feu aux Poudres*), painted in the same year, shows three cherubs swarming around another naked girl, who is sprawled on her disordered bed. One cherub raises the girl's bed sheet to expose her, a second, who is laid by her leg with his head near her foot, appears to have his own foot squarely nestled between her upper thighs. Her abandoned demeanour suggests that either she is in the grip of an erotic reverie or is enjoying a post-orgasmic lassitude. We may note that Fragonard's *Birth of Venus* of 1755 portrays the goddess as a plump society beauty, sprawled with thighs obligingly parted on billowing sheets, her cheeks and pouting lips a rosy pink. The same artist's *Venus Binding Cupid's Wings* (1753–1755) shows the pair kissing passionately whilst the goddess secures his pinions. In the context of these two images, a cupid arousing the love goddess seems an entirely possible scenario.

NUDE VENUS IN THE VICTORIAN ART

As the nineteenth century progressed, the relaxed attitude to nudes manifested by Boucher waned (in Britain certainly) and artists such as William Etty, who regularly painted female nudes, became oddities.

On the continent, life drawing was taught in the academies and nude paintings remained very popular. A picture such as Alexandre Cabanel's *Birth of Venus* (1863) exemplifies the French approach to nudes, with the goddess reclining languorously on a rock in the sea, surrounded by putti. *The Times* in 1869 declared that the artist had overstepped "the fine line which separates the sensuous from the sensual." The same might be said of William-Adolphe Bouguereau's *Birth of Venus* of 1879. The goddess stands on her scallop shell, luxuriously stretching her body and caressing her hair, whilst oceanids, tritons and putti surround her, celebrating her birth.

In Britain, the academic classical ideal was still recognised, but achieving it in a presentable form that could be exhibited and that did not violate middle-class respectable taste became an increasingly fraught enterprise. Representations of classical goddesses ought to have satisfied Victorian taste, but critics (and therefore the buying public) were constantly alert to anything in a painting that strayed from a depiction of the ideal and instead bore the signs of individuality. A canvas that suggested it portrayed an actual model would be sure to be condemned. The women who were prepared to remove their clothes for money in an artist's studio were perpetually equated with prostitutes and there was constant alarm over the risk that young men might be corrupted by viewing paintings of 'immoral' women.[4]

William Etty's drawing *Female Nude with a Cast of the Venus de Milo* (1833–37) illustrates the model to which young artists training at the Royal Academy and elsewhere aspired; it also highlights the problem that they faced. The art schools remained in thrall to the 'Old Masters' and the only way to keep nudity presentable seemed to be to try to make it as much like a marble statue as possible. Ironically, of course, this tactic is the reverse of what Pierre Louys employed in his *Aphrodite*. In that novel, temporal and geographical distance permitted him to depict bacchanalian excess and diverse sexualities more easily; for the Victorians, in contrast, the art of the Greek world was promoted as the pinnacle of pure aesthetics.

---

4 Alison Smith, *The Victorian Nude: Sexuality, morality and art*, 1996.

A great deal of moralising, hypocritical and sexist nonsense was written on this whole subject during the mid to late nineteenth century and artists continually walked a tightrope. On the one hand, in 1867 *Blackwood's Magazine* could declare that "All artists agree that the human form in its utmost simplicity, and especially the female form… is the very acme of all beauty." At this time the 'classical' paintings of Leighton, Poynter, Alma-Tadema and others were coming into favour, their nudes to a large degree rendered acceptable and permissible by the fact that they were safely located in ancient Greece, *not* in a present-day studio in St John's Wood. Leighton's *Venus Disrobing* of 1867 was praised because it rejected "corrupting Roman notions respecting Venus" (despite the painting's name!) Instead, the artist had "wisely reverted to the Greek idea of Aphrodite, a goddess worshipped, and by artists painted, as the perfection of female grace and beauty." By making his figure static and alone, presenting her as an 'abstract form,' Leighton steered clear of any possible suggestion of impropriety and won wide praise. The reviewer's distinction between a 'corrupt' Roman and 'pure' Grecian goddess is, as we now know, utterly fictitious.[5]

Character and situation in paintings were to be avoided. Art and photography critic Alfred H. Wall set this out in 1864:

> "The sensual vices, which we find in the fables of pagan priests and poets, have no more to do with these beautiful forms than with the names by which they were distinguished. The man who has a lovely wife, and calls her a 'perfect Venus,' does not thereby imply that she is an immoral character. He has in view the Venus of Grecian sculpture rather than the Venus of pagan mythology… The story of the fabled Venus as a goddess simply disgusts, but her sculptured form refines, delights and ennobles to this very day."[6]

---

5 *Art Journal,* June 1867.
6 A.H. Wall, 'On Studying from Nature,' *The Art Student,* December 1864.

One decade previously, critics had voiced concern about any painting that suggested paganism. Slowly, it became possible to view classical-style images for their formal beauty alone, divorced from the attendant mythology. Thus, F.G. Stephens praised Leighton's *Venus Disrobing* because there was no trace in it of the "languid, feverous and luxurious dame of love." A higher ideal had been attained: "Nakedness is not the leading characteristic of this figure; that sense must be very dull indeed and very coarse." Doubtless a similar reaction would have greeted Henrietta Rae's *Venus Enthroned*, completed in 1905. The goddess sits naked on her throne, surrounded only by flowers and doves. She is a full-breasted woman, but her contemplative, downcast gaze and decorously crossed legs avoid any hint of narrative or individual character. By contrast, when Matthew Hale exhibited *Psyche at the Throne of Venus* in 1879, the *Magazine of Art* condemned his "belle of the London streets with canary-coloured hair and blackened eyelashes." In Hale's dramatic scene, the bare-breasted goddess surveys the cowering nymph coldly and contemptuously; she is a mature woman, aware of her power and the fear she instils. She was too real, too 'naked.' Something similar happened to Royal Academician Sir Edward Poynter. He painted a Venus *Diadumene* in 1885. It showed a completely naked woman about to enter the pool of a Roman bath and attracted considerable adverse commentary. So controversial was the picture, in fact, that he was unable to sell it and had to add a robe, covering her legs and lower body, in 1893 – after which it was soon sold to a collector in the USA. Bared breasts were acceptable apparently – as, oddly, was the adolescent nude. In 1894 Poynter painted *Idle Fears*, a picture closely resembling *Diadumene*, which shows a naked girl of twelve or thirteen huddling against her mother rather than stepping into the water. Admittedly, we see her from behind, although the same artist's *Outward Bound* of 1886 is a more revealing image of a young adolescent, another scene which –

for no clear reason – was also deemed entirely acceptable to the public.

Much more fortunate was Albert Moore, who exhibited *A Venus* in 1869. This was a rendering of the *Venus de Milo*, and his strangely muscular, hairless and characterless figure was again praised for being "pure art and not historic or dramatic interest." Moore had painted an ideal, not an actual person (or goddess). In fact, some critics disliked the picture because it was *too* much like a cold statue and lacked any rose-tinted suggestion of flesh.[7]

There was no winning. In 1862 John Gibson exhibited a *Tinted Venus*, but his imitation of how classical Greek statues probably actually looked was rejected as improper. "We consider the adjunct of colour... as a departure from the high purpose of sculpture, which never aimed at more than an abstract type of subject represented in form and expression; its end being to idealise rather than to realise" complained the *Art Journal*.

Imitations of classical statues were quite popular as a way, perhaps, of heading off possible criticism. For instance, Whistler's drawing of *Venus* of 1869 – an unobjectionable image in any case as her arm covers her bosom and her legs and the twist of her body conceal her groin – is an homage to the *Cnidian Venus*. Whistler also drew a chalk and pastel sketch of *Venus Astarte*, an image which, by its name, might excite anticipation of a more sensual goddess. However, as Jeremy Maas commented, "the essence of classical beauty is achieved." Just like the previous drawing, the result is almost entirely sexless.[8]

Some artists dared to produce works that challenged the sanctimonious strictures of the British art establishment. Dante Gabriel Rossetti's *Venus Verticordia* is one such. The goddess is, as one might expect from Rossetti, a smouldering redhead, with full, luscious lips, who is seen surrounded by a lush profusion of

---

7 *Art Journal*, June 1861; *Athenaeum*, May 4th 1867; *The Globe*, 1869.
8 Maas, *Victorian Painters*, 1969.

berries and flowers – honeysuckle and roses. She has a golden halo, edged with butterflies, and fixes us with her intense blue eyes whilst holding an arrow and an apple. Publicly, Rossetti stated that her name derived from the goddess' power "to turn the hearts of women to cultivate chastity." This may have been what Lempriere's *Classical Dictionary* had told him, but whatever his inspiration, chastity is not a term readily associated with the painting (or with the Greek original). The arrow head hovering by the bared breast seems highly suggestive.

Worthy of mention too is Herbert James Draper's *Pearls of Aphrodite* of 1907. The goddess stands on a small rock in a cove, being offered pearls from the sea by her handmaidens. She casts back her cloak and robe to fasten a string around her neck; her attendant nymphs look on adoringly. These servants to the goddess remind us of another strong theme that continued to run through these scenes: the nymph or goddess as small breasted juvenile. Draper's awed innocents with chaplets of flowers woven into their hair are a good example; so too are George Frederick Watt's demure adolescent *Psyche* of 1880, a shy young teenager who avoids the viewer's gaze by lowering her eyes to the floor, Edward Burne-Jones slender *Venus Epithalamia* (1871) and William Stott's *Birth of Venus*, exhibited in 1887. The *Manchester Guardian* complained of the latter that, "instead of a goddess, [he] has given us a red-haired topsy." Emerging from what appear to be the steel grey waves of an icy North Sea beach, Stott's Venus is indeed a peculiar little creature, an oddly stiff and doll-like young girl with petite breasts and a wild mane of flaming hair. There is some echo of Botticelli, here, but only very faintly.

Stott's Venus may be compared to William Blake Richmond's *Aphrodite Between Eros & Himeros*, in which the goddess floats, startled and bemused, within a swirl of red hair. This vision of Aphrodite compares very poorly to that in Richmond's *Venus and Anchises* (1890): here, she is imperious and irresistible, striding radiantly through the countryside surrounded by doves and preceded by two lions. Anchises is awestruck and the look Venus gives him makes clear, as she starts to shed her robes, that he has little say over what's to follow. As we know, if you have been chosen as a lover by Venus, there's little point resisting or refusing her.

In 1903, Pierre Louys wrote an essay that reflected upon the hypocrisy of the contemporary attitudes of the art establishment.[9] He noted that Houdon's statue, *Diana the Huntress*, had been rejected by the Salon of 1777, its nudity being deemed indecent because it was too anatomically detailed. Louys first of all observed that it was a woman, Catherine the Great, who had eventually purchased the 'shocking' sculpture; then he examined the origins of classical statuary:

> "Some believe to be able to fix the origin of this tradition among the Greeks, from whom our art descends and is inspired. Rare, it is true, are the sexual Aphrodites: this is due first of all to the fact that the Greeks willingly represented the goddess in a naturally chaste attitude... Elsewhere, a first-rate statue from the best Greek period which we have – the excellent Alexandrian nude female replica popularly called the Venus of the Esquiline – would be enough to exonerate Houdon these days. Its anatomical truth is exact.
>
> And how many similar statues have been hammered to pieces by Christian vandalism! If the modest Venus were beheaded, what could not be done with the others! Those of the latter which have come down to us are almost all archaic because the land of oblivion already covered them and protected them at the time when the Roman St Polyeuctus massacred the goddesses even on the altars [he was an iconoclast and was martyred for it].

---

9 Louys, *The Statue of Truth*, 1902.

> The earthenware vases and statuettes that we find in the inviolate tombs leave us a better, more faithful and more complete testimony of what Greek art allowed from its origin to its decline."

Prudishness had nothing to do with Greek art, Louys concluded. More surprisingly, perhaps: "Natural Eve was carved on the portals of cathedrals." He dated prohibitions against realistic nudes as late as the reign of Louis XIII in France. Since then, he complained, what was allowed to ancient artists was no longer allowed to contemporaries, an unjustifiable situation – and one that was in the process of passing as he wrote.

SYMBOLIST GODDESSES

The painters of the Symbolist movement were particularly keen upon classical mythological scenes and made good use of the many gods, goddesses and other beings. Aphrodite and her sisters appear quite frequently in pictures. *The Birth of Venus* is a common scene, sometimes presented in slavish imitation of Botticelli, as with Walter Crane's canvas of 1877, *The Renaissance of Venus*. Doves flutter past, myrtle sprouts on the shore and the naked goddess tries to control her billowing hair, whilst looking down demurely to one side. Venus is an attractive young woman, but with quite a muscular frame. We might suppose that Crane wished to represent the intersex aspect of the goddess, but in fact the story goes that his wife objected to him working from naked female models, so he painted instead from an Italian called Alessandro di Marco, a young man popular with many London artists. Allegedly Lord Leighton spotted Alessandro's physique adapted to become Aphrodite when the picture was first exhibited at the Grosvenor Gallery.

French painter Gustave Moreau created some similarly conventional pictures: in his *Birth of Venus (Venus Appearing to*

Fishermen) the same long-haired, slender blonde beauty emerges from the waves and, in *Venus Rising from the Sea* (1866), she appears, arms outstretched to support her voluminous locks, whilst attendants offer her pearls and coral. Moreau's goddess is rather pallid and insipid, though, lacking Aphrodite's energy and power.

In contrast, Odilon Redon offers several sensually glowing visions of the same birth. The bright pink body of the goddess is revealed within a rosy heart of a shell, as if emerging from a womb (1866 and two from 1912). In a third canvas, dating from 1910, she sits at ease in a deep red shell, watching the breaking waves. In a fourth scene, also from 1912, she floats ashore in a giant nautilus shell.

Swiss Arnold Böcklin also tackled Venus' birth several times. His *Venus Anadyomene*, painted in 1872, is carried across the waves by a monstrous dolphin (another animal closely linked to the goddess in her marine aspects), whilst little cupids with butterfly wings flutter above her head, holding gauzy draperies around her. A *Birth of Venus* from 1869 rehearses the same scene, but with only a couple of cupids and the goddess' robes merging into what resembles a waterspout arising from the waves. Another such picture, also called the *Green Venus*, portrays the goddess walking on water. All of Böcklin's goddesses seem to be the same staid-looking Germanic matron, who is largely devoid of sexual frisson.

Sexuality was never far from the work of Aubrey Beardsley (1872–98). His *Venus Between Two Terminal Gods* (1895) depicts the goddess wearing a long, off-the-shoulder dress, with dark, tousled hair. She faces the viewer impassively, sternly even, as a dove glides in front of her. The statues on either side hold pan-pipes and carry baskets overflowing with fruit on their heads. This is a respectable, slightly intimidating deity, where as in *Eros and Aphrodite,* she is blatantly the harlot queen of physical love. We see her from behind, wearing only knee length stockings and reaching between her legs. Eros powders between her buttocks and thighs with a large soft brush, at the same time sporting a large erection; perhaps they are both excited by the titivations. The indications of incest and of a prostitute preparing herself for a client are typical of Beardsley's taste. Nonetheless, they are very much in the tradition of Bronzino and the mythology as well.

Symbolist style was adopted by society portraitist John Singer Sargent when he was asked to provide murals for Boston public library. His cycle, titled *The Triumph of Religion,* covers Egyptian and Assyrian religion as well Bible scenes portraying Judaism and Christianity. The work, on the hallway on the third floor of the McKim Building, occupied Sargent between 1890 and 1919.

Amongst the pagan gods the artist portrayed is a striking *Astarte,* painted in 1895, who wears a blue robe and stands upon a crescent moon. She is encrusted with beads and gold ornamentation highly reminiscent of Gustav Klimt. Naked attendants surround her, their hands raised in worship. Her eyes are closed and her lips bear a beatific smile. She is serene and powerful, sparkling with light, and is arguably a great deal more attractive a figure than the rather worthy 'Mysteries of the Rosary,' 'Dogma of Redemption,' 'Israelites Oppressed' or 'Prophets.'[10]

Within the Symbolist style, we might almost identify a separate genre of pictures, those that drew their inspiration from the myth of Tannhäuser. I mentioned Swinburne's poem on the subject, *Laus Veneris,* earlier. Edward Burne Jones took the poem's title for a painting of 1875, which shows Venus slumped in post-coital languor whilst her handmaidens play to her. Art historian Lionel Lambourne has observed that "the

---

[10] Note that Edgar Allen Poe in his poem *Eulalie* equates Astarte with the planet Venus and in *Ulalume,* the moon is Astarte's "bediamonded crescent/ Distinct with its duplicate horn."

painting carries a strikingly Freudian implication; the placing of a crown upon the lap of Venus, almost literally crowning the *mons Veneris*, was criticised by the *Spectator* as being obscure: 'when we do arrive at the meaning, it is not one we would care to explain to child or wife. The weariness of satisfied love, and the pain of unsatisfied longing, is hardly a theme, perhaps, to expend such a magnificent painting upon.'" Perhaps, but many other artists did just this.[11]

The legend of the Venusberg is a fascinating one. It seems to symbolise a longing for the old pagan faith and it also integrates Germanic myth into the classical legends. Venus is the goddess or faery queen who now seduces Tannhäuser into a life of sensual indulgence, but before the late Middle Ages she was called Hörsel, Hulda or Berchta. These elves or minor divinities appear to be aspects of Freja, the benevolent goddess of love, marriage and childbirth and the guardian of maidens – in many respects, a northern form of Aphrodite.

For painters, the sexy seductress Venus was too good a subject to ignore – and most paintings did not suffer the fault of 'obscurity' as did Burne Jones' *Laus Veneris*. In Gabriel Max's *Tannhäuser*, the goddess leans back against the young knight, throwing one arm around his shoulders whilst looking yearningly into his eyes. Her robe slips away from her torso, revealing her golden girdle round her waist. John Collier's 1901 *Venusberg* shows a more imperious deity, sitting topless on her throne with doves fluttering around her. She has her arms raised above her head, about to crown the kneeling, praying knight with a garland. The pose emphasises her breasts – and a naked girl stands to one side, just to underline the pleasures of the faery court that await him. Laurence Koe's *Venus and Tannhäuser* (1896) shows an even more wanton and seductive Venus, writhing nakedly on a bed of roses whilst the knight vainly seeks to focus on higher things. The Belgian Egide Rombaux's

---
11 Lambourne, *Victorian Painting*, 1999, 454.

sculpture, *Venusberg,* of about 1901, takes the eroticism yet further with three naked maidens engaged in a writhing and ecstatic dance.

EXPRESSIONIST EROS

As an icon of western art, Venus appealed to the German Expressionist painters, although their visions of her tended to be dark or simply brutally realistic. Some fairly conventional images were produced, but some lesser-known aspects of her character were also explored.[12]

A familiar wanton Venus is to be seen well portrayed in Lovis Corinth's illustrations for the 1919 edition of Schiller's erotic poem *Der Venuswagen:* the chariot or carriage of the title is "the whore's wagon," in which travels the nymphomaniac "Cyprian harlot."[13] In one scene depicted by Corinth, a smiling Venus reveals herself to us, surrounded by cupids, prancing satyrs, doves and two tigers; in another of the plates, Europa sits astride Zeus in bull form, beaming at us as she cradles her breasts in her hands. The easy confidence of the goddess in Corinth's illustrations is not mirrored by Otto Dix's *Venus with Black Gloves,* painted in 1932, which starkly sets a young girl against a plain black backdrop. She sits on a fur, awkwardly naked except for those elbow length gloves. Her hands clasp nervously at some fabric which is loosely draped around her hips and upper thighs; she looks exposed and unhappy. George Grosz's *Ländliche Venus* ('Rural Venus'), which was painted in 1945, is another complete contrast: she is a mature bodied country woman wearing just a headscarf, socks and shoes, who seems the epitome of the

---

12 Examples might be Kees van Dongen's nude Venus, Max Pechstein's nude in a sea shell or Lovis Corinth's *Birth of Venus* and *Mirror of Venus.*

13 This volume was the first of a series of nine issued by Fritz Gurlitt Verlag in Berlin between 1919 and 1920. It featured erotic prints; other volumes included Victor-Joseph Étienne de Jouy's *Sappho or the lesbians* and *The Royal Orgy, or, the Austrian Woman in a Good Mood: An Opera.*

maternal female. Georg Tappert's *Venus von Milo* (1918) is another such voluptuous and mature nude. Paula Modersohn-Becker painted a variation on this theme in her still life *Small Venus Bust and Apricot* (1906). In the foreground is a small white bust of the goddess and an apricot; behind them Becker has painted a half-length image of herself, nude and pregnant, set on a pedestal, before which lies a much larger apricot, with the fruit painted so as to emphasise its resemblance to female genitalia. The image communicates the themes of sexuality and fertility even more strongly than those already described. The work of many of the Expressionists was later to be condemned by the Nazis as degenerate, so that it is interesting to contrast these pictures of real, natural and healthy German women with Sepp Hilz's 1939 *Bäuerliche Venus* ('Peasant Venus'), in which an ideal Aryan maiden adopts a classic pose associated with Greek statues of Aphrodite, standing on one leg to pull on her slipper. Joseph Goebbels provided an endorsement of this Germanic Venus by purchasing the canvas when it was exhibited in 1942.

Another side to the goddess is seen in Max Bechmann's *Venus und Mars*, painted in 1945. The god kneels, aiming a bow and arrow, and awaiting the command to fire from a Venus who wears a Napoleonic era military uniform – albeit with bare breasts. In diametrical opposition to this image is Raoul Dufy's *Aphrodite aux Papillons* (1938). The sturdy looking goddess reclines on a shell, a wash of blue suggesting the sea behind her. Above her, three bright butterflies are fluttering; these insects aren't directly linked to her cult, but they are related to the nymph Psyche, lover of Eros, of whose beauty Aphrodite was jealous. You may recall that butterflies hover, too, about Rossetti's *Venus Verticordia*.

The last Expressionist image to consider is Oskar Kokoschka's *Alma Doll as Venus*. In 1919 the painter had a friend create for him a life-sized female doll that was modelled on his former lover, the widow of Gustav Mahler. This bizarre construction was planned to have cotton wool buttocks and breasts, so that the artist would be able to 'cuddle' her. In the end, the pneumatic model was covered in feathers, which made it hard for Kokoschka to dress and handle her as he'd planned; nevertheless, he used to pose the mannequin and then photograph or paint her. In the *Venus* image of the Alma doll, she reclines on a sofa, her head resting on her left hand, her right arm extended along her body, rather like the recumbent Venuses of Giorgione or Titian. With her exaggerated curves, large breasts and fixed eyes, she is a weird, downy and very disturbing sex toy. It may come as little surprise that the Nazis also considered Kokoschka's art degenerate, but the doll might be seen as confirmation that Aphrodite can embrace all sexualities. She can represent fecundity and reproduction, but she can also symbolise a diversity of pleasures.

SALVADOR DALI

Salvador Dali is probably the most famous surrealist artist, although many would argue that he hitched a ride on the movement to benefit his career. He created several significant works dealing with the goddess of love, but she was already a person of interest to the movement. For example, in 1929, the last issue of the journal *La Revolution surrealiste* featured a full-page photomontage created by Rene Magritte. At its centre was an image of a naked woman that is very clearly derived from Botticelli's *Birth of Venus* or from the *Medici Venus*. She stands covering her breast and looks modestly to one side; she symbolises the key word in a phrase printed around her: "*Je ne vois pas la [femme] cachée dans la fôret*" (I can't see the woman hidden in the forest). The image is framed by photobooth pictures of sixteen of the leading surrealist (male) artists, such as Andre Breton, Max Ernst and Dali, all with their eyes shut.

It's tempting to see this as a mild chauvinist joke, but it has been argued that the image is far more significant than that.[14]

The issue of *La Revolution surrealiste* in which the picture appeared was mainly concerned with an 'Inquiry into Love,' as part of which painters and writers had been asked to respond to a series of questions on the subject. One element in surrealist thought was the medieval idea of 'courtly love,' the longing for a noble lady who is adored as a distant and abstract ideal. It has been proposed that Magritte's Venus must be viewed this way. Her figure is an abstract concept, personifying idealised and unattainable love; she is more than just a nude, an object. She also represents a challenge to the simple idea of 'love as happiness.' As the medieval bards and singers knew, there can be pain in finding love and in loving; it can be a masochistic experience. That's why the men in Magritte's picture all have their eyes shut: they're still searching for their individual Venus. Indeed, Andre Breton's lover, Suzanne Muzard, responded to the 'love survey' conducted by the magazine in terms he wholly endorsed: love was, she said, about the discovery of an indispensable person – "There is a great mystery in finding. Nothing can be compared to the fact of loving."

However we might interpret them, nudes in classical landscapes nevertheless lay at the core of pre-war surrealism, as may be seen in the work of Italian Giorgio de Chirico and Belgian painter Paul Delvaux. The latter's 1944 painting, *Sleeping Venus,* is very typical of his style. The goddess lies on a bed in a town square amidst colonnaded buildings; near her various other naked women raise their arms in distress, perhaps because a skeleton and a mysterious woman in late nineteenth century dress and hat are approaching the recumbent figure. Delvaux himself said that the picture reflected the alarm and fear of living through wartime bombing.

---

14 *La Revolution surrealiste*, no.12, December 1929; D. Bate, *Photography & Surrealism,* 2004, 148–171.

Returning to Salvador Dali, early in his artistic career the young Spanish artist painted a fairly conventional *Venus and Cupids* (1925), and several versions of *Venus and a Sailor,* in which the goddess resembles a huge classical statue but is posed as a port town prostitute, waiting for her seafarer to return home. Dali's vision of the goddess fully took flight when, in 1938 at the Galerie Beaux-Arts in Paris, and subsequently at the 1939 World's Fair in New York, he created the *Dream of Venus* pavilion, bringing surrealist art to a wider audience. This display was a very early example of a multi-media installation, with sound, performance and the architecture itself contributing to the overall effect. The pavilion included an aquarium in which seventeen mermaids swam around in a submerged living room. In this underwater lounge these 'Living Liquid Ladies' had a roaring fire, telephones and a typewriter. Another woman was dressed in a black rubber costume painted with piano keys, which the mermaids would 'play.'

Outside, sculpted mermaids, bathing belles and coral adorned the façade, which looked something like a bright white sandcastle. The ticket office was a fish's head and customers then entered between a pair of woman's legs in striped socks, over which there stood Botticelli's goddess from his *Birth of Venus*.

Internally, the walls were covered with reproductions of Dali's paintings turned into wallpaper and there were fantastical furniture and objects, such as Venus herself, asleep topless on a red satin bed thirty-six feet (eleven metres) long. A recording voiced Venus' dreams aloud: "In the fever of love, I lie upon my ardent bed – a bed eternally long – and I dream my burning dreams; the longest dreams ever dreamed, without beginning and without end…. Enter the shell of my house and you will see my dreams." In a mirror beside Venus, it was possible to see her dreams enacted: a bare-breasted woman with crossed arms wore a massive bouquet of geraniums over her face and head.

She twitched and shook, apparently trying to escape. Behind the bed, there was an oval cut-out in the headboard, a window onto the adjacent wet tank, suggesting that the aquarium and the mermaids also represented the depths of Venus' unconscious and her dream. Another bare breasted woman would appear from time to time behind the bed, shushing visitors so as not to wake the slumbering goddess.

Other exhibits in the pavilion included a corridor roofed with umbrellas and a room containing Dali's 'Rainy Taxi,' a vehicle covered in ivy, driven by a dummy and with models sprawled on the bonnet. Venus, the mermaids and the other models were all topless, although in some of the publicity photographs bunches of flowers discreetly cover their breasts.

This entire exhibit is very typical of Surrealist art, in which objects are combined unexpectedly, in disorientating surroundings, with the aim of jolting the observer into new ways of seeing. The emphasis on the dreams of Venus reflects the interest of the movement in the theories of Freud on the unconscious and its expression. That said, the emphasis on young women semi-naked is also quite typical of the rather sexist attitudes of the (mainly) male movement. Venus, of course, is co-opted because of her very association with sexuality and (from one perspective) the satisfaction of male desire. This chauvinist appropriation of her means that she was present only to be displayed with her tits out – a thrill in the 1930s that was doubled by the mirrors behind her bed. Otherwise, Venus was passive and asleep.

Dali didn't leave the love goddess there, though. His *Venus de Milo with Drawers* (1936) is an "anthropomorphic cabinet" with drawers – equipped with fluffy pompom handles – fitted into her forehead, breasts, stomach, abdomen, and left knee. This statue embodies the Surrealist principles of combining unlikely elements to surprise and disorientate the viewer, although the main response may be mild amusement. It is arguable, too, that the piece once again demonstrates a sexist objectification of women. It is demeaning not just to the goddess but to females more generally

The artist painted an *Apparition After the Aphrodite of Cnidus* in 1981, in which the famous statue's impassive face appears superimposed upon a slab of stone floating above a landscape. His heliogravure and dry-point of 1963, *Aphrodite,* presents the viewer with a far more challenging and thought-provoking image than the previous two examples. The pose of the subject's statuesque body recalls that of Botticelli's Venus: she stands on a scallop with her hair billowing behind her. However, she is pierced by nails, in her face, neck, armpit, nipples, abdomen and thigh, in response to which, perhaps, one hand is clenched like a claw. At the same time, the figure is threatened by dark swirling storm clouds and a very large phallus.

PAUL CUVELIER

Cuvelier was born in 1923 in Lens, near Mons, in Belgium. From a young age he showed a very precocious talent for art, often making drawings and paintings outdoors and illustrating stories for his siblings. He became one of the original contributors to *Tintin* magazine, working as an illustrator from its start in 1946 until the early 1970s. However, Cuvelier is best-known for his historical adventure series about young *Corentin* (1946–1974), in addition to which he also drew the investigations of the young woman *Line* (1962–1972) and the ground-breaking erotic graphic novel *Epoxy* (1968). Cuvelier's graphic novel output was, however, characterised by long intervals of inactivity. He continually drifted between his ambitions as a fine artist and the more financially rewarding comics industry, which resulted in a rather fragmented and unstable record in both. The connecting thread between his activities in these two art forms remained his fascination for the aesthetics of human anatomy.

The artist saw comics as a necessary way to earn money, but his true passion lay in painting and sculpture, especially female nudes, which showcased his passion for the life drawing. Cuvelier's fine art was characterised by a sensuality which has been described as "slumbering eroticism," although – in fact – exactly the same could be said about some of the art work in his comics.

In 1973 Cuvelier brought the *Corentin* series to an end and decided thereafter to focus upon fine art. He had found cartoons too restrictive and wished to dedicate himself to what has been called his 'artistic adventure,' whatever the commercial risks involved. During the same year, he met his last model, an eighteen-year-old called Brigitte, who was to be immensely inspiring for him during his final years. She has been described by one authority on Cuvelier as being a 'sprig' of an adult woman, with an adolescent body, candid looks and a tart mixture of instinctive femininity and natural childishness. In some sense, she was his cartoon character *Line* incarnated, combining the mysterious charm and provoking seductiveness that Cuvelier had sought to express in many of his drawings of young females.[15]

Paul Cuvelier's final output included some erotic illustrations for *Privé* magazine in 1975, but he then received the ideal commission – to prepare a special *ex libris* collection of drawings for the *Cercle des Bibliophiles*. The theme settled upon was 'nymphets' or 'apprentice Aphrodites.' This subject matter was perfect for Cuvelier. Throughout his career he had drawn female nudes, frequently large breasted women but quite often lesbian couples entwined or fetish images of women in leather boots or elbow length gloves. Whatever the exact form the images took, as critic Philippe Goddin has written, Cuvelier was always obsessed with an 'ideal beauty' and, in particular, was 'engrossed

---

15 Philippe Goddin, *Paul Cuvelier – L'Aventure Artistique*, Magic Strip, 33; this was also published in Flemish as *Jonge Afrodites*.

by the contemplation of youthful anatomy.' This was because, Goddin said, "These bodies have not yet suffered the attrition of life or of time. Adolescent forms captivated him." The artist himself was in poor health and may well have envied his young models' youth and vitality.[16]

For the 1977 commission, Brigitte was the ideal model. She has been described as possessing "an undecided adolescence, divided between the attractions of womanhood and the inclination to prolong her infancy." Cuvelier was said to have been amazed and intrigued by the contradictions in his model's character: her "purity, freshness and candour, tinged with seduction ... her tenderness, sensuality, the emotion of discovery, the privilege of the moment." Whatever the exact nature of their personal interaction, his artistic response is clear: she directly and materially inspired Cuvelier's final triumph, giving rise to large numbers of sketches of "virginal reveries, juvenile outbursts and adolescent high-spirits." Cuvelier's published illustrations of *'fillettes'* (little girls) or *'jeunes Aphrodites'* are regarded by many as the finest expression of his sensibility and technical ability, the peak achievement of his "profound interrogation of the female form."[17]

Amongst this later work there are some faux classical *'centauresses,'* juvenile female centaurs who are cute and amusing; there are also some very free sketches of Brigitte posing in underwear, boots and varying degrees of undress. However, it was his works in oils and watercolours for the collector's edition 'Aphrodites' that must be regarded Cuvelier's true triumph and memorial.

The plates for the dual language edition of *Jeunes Aphrodites/ Jonge Afrodites* depict a collection of girls and young women of various ages, but the most notable pictures feature girls aged about eleven or twelve, perhaps, naked or partially clothed.

---
16 Goddin, *Cuvelier – Les Chemins du Merveilleux*, 2006, 8–10.
17 Goddin, *L'Aventure*, 44 & 49.

They are sometimes alone, sometimes in pairs. Some of these images don't depict 'Aphrodites' as such, but they bear a clear sexual charge. A naked girl stands with her legs apart, wearing only white calf-length boots and an orange bow in her hair. She covers her face and groin with her hands – possibly in mock embarrassment. Another picture captures a nude blonde balancing on one foot as she slips off her pink knickers – perhaps a modern echo of Venus fastening her sandal. In a third plate, a 'gipsy' girl with dark hair is seen in the process of pulling her dress off over her head, leaving her naked except for grey socks.

The 'young lesbian' pictures drawn for the Aphrodite collection are the most deliberately erotic, yet they are also hardest to read. The girls are seen to be involved in some sort of interaction – they are in the process of undressing, admiring each other, perhaps preparatory for their first tentative same-sex contact. In one scene, a girl in a short vest, straw hat and socks and sandals raises the top worn by her otherwise naked friend, gazing at her friend's groin in rapt fascination. These are novice examples of the female lovers Cuvelier had so often depicted previously. The 1977 collection includes several plates showing young women in their late teens or early twenties in loving embraces, but the pictures of the younger pair are amongst Cuvelier's most polished and intriguing images, without a doubt.

Amongst all these plates, there are just a few which more directly evoke Aphrodite. One illustration shows a girl of eleven or twelve standing on a crate, with her dress in folds around her feet. Her left hand is raised to the shoulder, her other arm is crossed over her eyes. Her pose overall subtly imitates a classical statue. A second plate comprises four separate images of young girls standing on a sea shore, looking away from us out to sea. They are all naked, so these are primarily studies on long hair and shapely backs, buttocks and legs. The weather is different in each frame: in one a blonde girl faces a very black and stormy sky and her hair is whipped about by the wind. In another, a second blonde girl stands in front of a very large scallop shell, a very clear reference to Botticelli's Venus and to the ostensible theme of the entire book.

Cuvelier's 'Young Aphrodites' are a further and logical development of the pictorial ideas of Boucher and some of the Expressionists – and of the intellectual conception of the goddess developed by fellow Belgian, Pierre Louys. Sexuality is ever-present, but it is far more liberated and diverse than was the case in the past. Many of Cuvelier's young goddesses want to have sex with each other, not with the artist or the viewer. Equally, their sexual attraction and potential is stressed, whatever their age. The sexuality of the goddess is not to be restrained by arbitrary limits.

It seemed that Cuvelier was so inspired by this commission that he planned more work on the same theme. Sadly, however, he died in 1978 in Charleroi, aged only 54, after years of declining health which had been aggravated by mental health problems, poverty and homelessness.

Conclusion

> "Honour the god who is by far the sweetest to mortals – Aphrodite."[1]

Over the millennia, Venus-Aphrodite has performed many roles. She has been the bringer of Spring, guardian of seafarers, divine mother and, even, cleanser of sewers. Her core interest, inspiring love and sex, has persisted throughout and remains as vital today as it was in the ancient world.

Poet Geoffrey Grigson commented upon the nature of Aphrodite's persistence:

> "Answering our needs, offspring of our wants, our desires, our hopes, our dread, our insecurity, our insufficiencies and uncertainties, our fancies, gods in the West came slowly to mature personification. Then they died slowly. But even their death was often incomplete. Something of the old god survived in a new god, in a new personification, persuasively introduced and answering, under a new name, to mutations and alterations in the human condition … It was hard for such a goddess to die altogether. All the time her circumstances remain in the relations of men and women. She comes back."[2]

Inanna became Ishtar, became Astarte, became Aphrodite, became Venus, became Mary, but survived all along – because she met our deepest desires.

---

1 Euripides, *Alkestis*, lines 790–91.
2 Grigson, *The Goddess of Love*, 19.

CONCLUSION

Aphrodite symbolises everything uninhibited and spontaneous about human passion. She has had numerous lovers, human *and* divine; she has gone in pursuit of those partners, unrestricted by any conceptions of the conventional passive female role. Whilst there doesn't seem to be any record of Venus herself taking same sex lovers, her cult made it clear that all love was good; that all pleasure with a partner, whoever that might be, was welcomed enthusiastically as a sacrament to her. It's worth recalling here the boy Adonis who became her lover; he was also Apollo's partner, underlining the 'free love' aspects of her cult. An aspect of Aphrodite could be found condoning nearly everything: incest, sex with younger partners, anal intercourse, enjoyment of sex toys and paid-for pleasure with sex workers. The Victorian addition of BDSM adds little to what the Greeks had already accepted.

This unashamed celebration of the joys of the body – your own and others' – remains the resonant and uplifting message of the queen of love. Humans are given their bodies in order to enjoy delight and thereby to worship the goddess. Aphrodite encourages and endorses all acts of adoration between lovers as adoration of her. Historian Monica Cyrino reminds us of the goddess amazingly diverse nature: she is "a polyvalent deity, plural in nature but never fragmented."[3]

Aphrodite continues to be alive and present for many. She is still worshipped and invoked.[4] She can still bring help and hope in matters of love and sexuality.[5] But, even if we don't feel the need to seek the help of the goddess, we can still feel her

---

[3] M. Cyrino, *Aphrodite*, 2010, 5.

[4] See, for example, Laurelei Black, *The Cult of Aphrodite – The Rites & Festivals of the Golden One*, which is a liturgical compilation (2010).

[5] For instance, Dave Thompson, *Grecian Magick – the Magick of Aphrodite, Apollo & Hermes*, 2021; Chelsea Wakefield, *In Search of Aphrodite – Women, Archetypes & Sex Therapy*, 2015; Jane Meredith, *Aphrodite's Magic – Celebrate & Heal Your Sexuality*, 2009; Joanne Brun, *Aphrodite's Secrets: Dressing Up for Getting Down and Other Ways to Unleash Your Inner Sex Goddess*, 2004, or Isabel Allende, *Aphrodite – love of food & food love*, 2005.

immanence, as Geoffrey Grigson suggested, through the flowers, fruit and creatures associated with her:

> "If we look at them and experience them for ourselves, we can, I think, achieve some special rapport, after all these centuries, with the goddess and with the feelings and needs she personified ... There is a reciprocity here: if the roses we pick in our own gardens, without going to Greece or Cyprus or the Lebanon, tell us something about Aphrodite, in turn the contemplation of Aphrodite tells us something extra about [them]."[6]

Aphrodite has her faults but, ultimately, what makes her attractive to us still are her essential qualities: love, liberality and acceptance. These represent her deep appeal and explain why she should still be celebrated.

We want our gods to understand us and to answer our prayers. Aphrodite does this: she shares our passions; she relishes our pleasures as her own. She is endlessly mutable, evolving with society whilst yet having seen it all. For all these reasons, she is the modern goddess of love.

---

6 Grigson, *The Goddess of Love*, 184.

Lightning Source UK Ltd.
Milton Keynes UK
UKHW021117201021
392517UK00004B/36